A SINGLE GIRL'S GUIDE TO...

Hilarious Facts You Never Knew About Sex

A SINGLE GIRL'S GUIDE TO...

Hilarious Facts You Never Knew About Sex

Sarah Melland

Copyright © 2020 Sarah Melland
Published by Ripe Melland Media

All rights reserved. No part of this publication may be reproduced, stored in a retrieval system, or transmitted, in any form or by any means, electronic, mechanical, photocopying, recording, or otherwise, without the prior written permission of the publisher.

ISBN: 978-1-7346333-8-2

CONTENTS

1. Shut Up and Kiss Me — 1
2. Take It in The Mouth — 20
3. Don't Be Silly Protect Your Willie — 28
4. Why Say Lubricant ...When You Can Say LubriCAN! — 43
5. I Want Your Sex, Baby — 48
6. I Think It's Time We Talk About Sex Toys — 68
7. There She Blows, There She Blows Again — 76
8. Everybody Masturbates Sometimes — 111

1.
Shut Up and Kiss Me

We have all had them. The terrible kisser. The sloppy, engulf mouth-spitter. There are some men, right when they kiss you, you want to drop your panties instantly and see what they can do down below.

I will admit, sometimes you just don't mesh well together. I am not going to say guys are bad kissers, I just don't like really wet kisses and a slobbery mouth. I can't. I just can't. So, I found there are thirty different kissing techniques to use through the Kama Sutra, so you will never be a bad kisser again, and make guys wanting more. And yes, some men I will teach if they are coachable, and worthy of my time.

THE KAMA SUTRA'S 30 KISSING TECHNIQUES

Askew kiss. When the heads of the two are tilted in opposite directions and then plant one on each other. Heads bowed allow better contact of the lips and a deep penetration of the tongue. This is the most popular, I'm pretty sure.

Bent kiss. When one of the two throws their head back and the other holding it over their chin and kisses them.

The sweetness and affection are the main emotions that are transmitted with this kiss. A kiss of this kind is appropriate for the preliminaries.

Direct kiss. When the lips of both bind directly and suck as if it were a ripe fruit. It is a kind of kiss where what matters are the lips that suck, nibble and caress it gently with the tongue. Reposado is a long kiss, which may express a strong passion and that many people are excited more than a kiss with tongue.

Kiss pressure. The lips are pressed tightly with your mouth closed. A kiss to start or to end the relationship, should not keep for long. The teeth are stuck on the inside of the mouth and can leave blood.

Top kiss. When one of the two teeth taken with the upper lip and the other returned the kiss kissing the lower lip. In the description of this kiss is said that one takes the initiative and the other is limited to respond, possibly because the Kamasutra was written for an active and passive. Everyone should be as creative as possible and let your imagination be shown and is expressed as it is, and not simply respond to the initiative of another.

Kiss clip. When the tongue touches the teeth, gums, tongue or palate of the other, called "Fight of the tongue." In my opinion, this sounds sloppy.

Throbbing kiss. When one of the two deposited over thousands of kissing lips very young traveling across the mouth and the corners. One partner kisses the other partner sweetly.

Contact kiss. When the tongue lightly touches the other's mouth and barely touches the partner's lips.

Kiss to ignite. The flame is the kiss at the corners of the mouth that usually occurs in the middle of the night to kindle love, that looks innocent but may not be.

Kiss to distract. When want to draw your attention to your kisses. For starters, remember that not all have to be kissing on the mouth. According to the Kamasutra, other recommended places to start the battle are the forehead, eyes, cheeks, throat, chest, nipples, the area inside the mouth, hairline, neck and neck with the clavicle.

Nominal kiss. When you simply touch the other's mouth, then kissing them with two fingers.

Kiss with your eyelashes. Touch and caress other person's lips lightly with your eyelashes.

Kiss with a finger. When the lover crosses the mouth of the beloved, inside and out with a finger.

Kiss with two fingers close. When the lover fingers, wetting them slightly and press the mouth of the beloved.

Kiss that awakens. The kiss that is given in the temples, near the hairline, while the other is asleep, to wake them gently.

Public Kiss. One of the two approaches the other and kissing him gently on the hand or neck.

The Kiss of Remembrance. This is when the lovers are resting satisfied with the passion and one of them puts their head on the thigh of the other and drops, as if asleep, kissing them on the thigh or great toe.

Transferred Kiss. Like teenagers kissing a poster on the wall, this kiss is when the lover, in the presence of the beloved, or a portrait or a picture or anything, looking for you to know that this kiss is for them. So, all those years kissing my pillow, the man of my dreams felt it?

Tearful kiss. Occurs when one of the two casts so much, the other that in its absence, kisses his portrait.

Kiss traveler. Although it seems kisses always tend to focus on the mouth, lips posing in other parts of the body is an exciting way guaranteed.

Kiss the breast. The most effective kisses on her nipples are first applied to the lips, gently and with a little saliva. Then the pressure intensifies, and if the couple wants and likes, you can take the nipple with a little teeth and pressing gently. Some people prefer to feel some pain in them when they are about to have an orgasm.

Kiss without a clock. The key is to pay full attention on each other's bodies. The more control you have and the more you concentrate on stroking and kissing every inch of the body, the stronger the feeling of pleasure for both.

Bites often occur in almost all parts of the body, ranging from the playful bite, more provocative than erotic, even the strong grip with the teeth that usually occurs at the peak of passion and makes orgasms more durable. However, many tend to avoid the latter type of bite because it is difficult to control and often leave marks evident. Also, because during orgasm jaws may suffer a spasm and close tightly, which can cause injury.

The bites are recommended by the Kama Sutra:

Bite of the Boar. The trail leaves the skin are as many rows of sharp markings, very close to each other, and with red intervals as the tracks that usually leaves the pigs in the mud. It is a bite that is often in the shoulder.

The stream tag. Consists of uneven skin surveys in a circle, produced by the spaces between teeth. The Kamasutra specifies that this type of bite should be in the chest.

Escondido Bite. The bite that only leaves a red mark and intense to be given in the lower lip.

Bite classic. When taken between the teeth a lot of skin.

The point. When taken between the teeth a small amount of skin so that only left a mark as a red dot.

Dashed line. When that little piece of skin is bitten with all the teeth and they all leave their mark. Should be on the forehead or thigh.

The coral and the jewel. The bite that results from coupling the teeth and lips. The lips are coral and teeth are the jewel.

Jewelry line. When biting down with all the teeth.

MY LIPS DON'T LIE

- ❖ A woman in China partially lost her hearing after her boyfriend reportedly ruptured her eardrum with a passionate kiss. Apparently, the kiss reduced the pressure in the mouth, pulled the eardrum out, and caused the breakdown of the ear.

- The insulting slang "kiss my ass" dates back at least to 1705.

- Lips are 100 times more sensitive than the tips of the fingers.

- Approximately two-thirds of people tip their head to the right when they kiss. Some scholars speculate this preference starts in the womb.

- The mouth is full of bacteria. When two people kiss, they exchange between 10 million and 1 billion germs. Cooties ☺

- The most important muscle in kissing is the orbicularis oris, also known as the kissing muscle. (The shape you make with your mouth mirrors that of a breastfeeding baby, hinting at one possible way that kissing evolved.) This muscle allows the lips to "pucker." Did you just pucker your lips? Cause I did.

- French kissing involves 34 facial muscles. A pucker kiss involves only two.

- The lips of both men and women resemble the lips of the vagina. I don't know why this is important, just in case you were unsure what a Delta of Venus looks like.

- The term "French kiss" came into the English language around 1923 as a slur on the French culture which was thought to be overly concerned with sex. In France, it's called a tongue kiss or soul kiss because if done right, it feels as if two souls are merging. In fact, several ancient cultures thought that mouth-to-mouth kissing mingled two lovers' souls.

❖ The Four Vedic Sanskrit texts (1500 B.C.) contain the first mention of a kiss in writing.

❖ The Romans created three categories of kissing: *Osculum*, a kiss on the cheek; *Basium*, a kiss on the lips; and *Savolium*, a deep kiss.

❖ Kissing for one-minute burns 26 calories.

❖ It is possible for a woman to reach an orgasm through kissing. (See orgasm portion of this book for more details.)

❖ Mechanically speaking, kissing is almost identical to suckling. Some scholars speculate that the way a person kisses may reflect whether he or she was breastfed or bottle fed.

❖ Kissing is good for teeth. The anticipation of a kiss increases the flow of saliva to the mouth, giving the teeth a plaque-dispersing bath.

❖ Scientists believe that kissing may be a way of exchanging body salts or sebum that form relationships with parents and lovers, just as it does some birds. During mating, some birds chew food, then kiss-feed it to a prospective mate. If a bird's sebaceous glands are removed so there is no sebum, its mate flies off.

❖ According to one study, many men are more particular about which women they kissed than who they went to bed with, suggesting that kissing is somehow more about love than putting the P in the V is.

- ❖ Kissing may have originated when mothers orally passed chewed solid food to their infants during weaning. Another theory suggests kissing evolved from prospective mates sniffing each other's pheromones for biological compatibility. Umm…when did mothers do this? Do I have to?

- ❖ Scholars are unsure if kissing is a learned or instinctual behavior. In some African and Asian cultures kissing does not seem to be practiced.

- ❖ Common chimpanzees kiss with open mouths, but not with their tongues. Bonobos, the most intelligent of primates, do kiss with their tongues.

- ❖ Leper-kissing became fashionable among medieval ascetics and religious nobility during the twelfth and thirteenth centuries. It was deemed proof of humility.

- ❖ During the Middle Ages, witches' souls were supposed to be initiated into the rites of the Devil by a series of kisses, including kissing the Devil's anus, which was a parody of kissing the Pope's foot.

- ❖ Pliny asserts that kissing a donkey's nostril will cure the common cold.

- ❖ Kissing at the conclusion of a wedding ceremony can be traced to ancient Roman tradition where a kiss was used to sign contract.

❖ The first on-screen kiss was shot in 1896 by the Edison Company. *The May Irwin-John C. Rice Kiss*, the film was 30 seconds long and consisted entirely of a man and a woman kissing close up.

❖ The first on-screen kiss between two members of the same sex was in Cecil B. DeMille's *1922 Manslaughter*.

❖ Under the Hays Code (1930-1968), people kissing in American films could no longer be horizontal; at least one had to be sitting or standing, not lying down. In addition, all on-screen married couples slept in twin beds, and if kissing on one of the beds occurred, at least one of the spouses had to have a foot on the floor.

❖ Polls consistently list the kiss between Ingrid Bergman and Cary Grant in the 1946 film *Notorious* as one of the sexiest kisses in cinematic history. Because the Hays Code allowed on-screen kisses to last only a few seconds, Alfred Hitchcock directed Bergman and Grant to repeatedly kiss briefly while Grant was answering a telephone call. The kiss seems to go on and on but was never longer than a few seconds.

❖ Kissing played an important role in ancient Greco-Roman culture and was seen as a sign of respect, thanks, reunion, and agreement, as well as a rite of inclusion. Kisses were exchanged between peers, political leaders, teachers, and priests. Hence, the kiss of Judas ("Kiss of Death") to betray Christ inverted the very point of kissing in this early Christian context.

- ❖ The film with the most kisses is *Don Juan* (1926) in which John Barrymore and Mary Astor share 127 kisses. The film with the longest kiss is Andy Warhol's 1963 film *Kiss*. The 1961 film *Splendor in the Grass*, with Natalie Wood and Warren Beatty, made history for containing Hollywood's first French kiss.

- ❖ Early Christians kissed one another in highly specific settings that distinguished them from the non-Christian population. The earliest Christian reference to the ritual kiss is at the end of I Thessalonians: "Greet one another with a holy kiss." The Christian ritual kiss or "kiss of peace" was used during prayer, Eucharist, baptism, ordination, and in connection with greeting, funerals, monastic vows, and martyrdom.

- ❖ Although many men and women consider it childish, more than 95 percent of them occasionally like to rub noses while kissing. Often called an "Eskimo kiss" in Western culture, this form of kissing is based loosely on a traditional Inuit greeting called a "kunik."

- ❖ In 1929, anthropologist Bronislaw Malinowski visited the Trobriand Islands to observe their sexual customs. He found that two lovers will go through several phases of sucking and biting in a variation of the French kiss that culminates in biting off each other's eyelashes. In fact, in the South Pacific, short eyelashes are a status symbol.

I don't think women with eyelash extensions would like that very much, but that is just my humble opinion.

❖ Diseases which can be transmitted through kissing include mononucleosis ("kissing disease") and herpes. Contracting HIV through kissing is extremely unlikely, though one woman was infected in 1997 when the woman and infected man both had gum disease. Transmission was likely through the man's blood and not his saliva.

❖ Rodin's famous statue *The Kiss* was originally titled *Francesca da Rimini* and depicts the thirteenth-century woman in Dante's *Inferno* who falls in love with her husband's younger brother Paolo. Their lips do not actually touch, hinting at their eventual doom.

❖ A medieval manuscript warns Japanese men against deep kissing during the female orgasm because a woman might accidentally bite off part of her lover's tongue.

❖ The kiss of life (breath of God) and the kiss of death (Judas' kiss) are powerful literary and artistic symbols. Sixteenth century authors were especially likely to use them as sexual metaphors.

❖ The average person spends at least two weeks of their life kissing.

❖ On July 16, 1439, King Henry VI banned kissing in England to prevent the spread of the plague.

- Over 400,000 tourists gather to kiss the Blarney Stone near Cork, Ireland every year, making it the "most unhygienic" tourists in the world.

- Our brains have special neurons that help us find each other's lips in the dark.

- "Basorexia" means an overwhelming desire to kiss.

- Kissing Can Help Boost Your Immune System. According to special research and study in physiology and behavior, researchers have found that kissing can improve our body's resistance to allergies.

- Your lips have a disproportionate number of nerve endings compared to other parts of your body. When your lips touch someone else's 5 out of 12 of your cranial nerves are engaged.

- More kissing in a relationship is related to how satisfied people say they are in that relationship.

- Your First Kiss Can Seal the Deal or Call It Off. When you kiss someone for the first time, you get a spike in the neurotransmitter dopamine, making you crave more. Dopamine can also make you lose your appetite and make it hard for you to sleep.

- Kissing Your Pet Can Cause Excessive Dental Bacteria.

- Over time, kissing lowers your levels of stress hormone cortisol, making you feel all safe and secure.

- When you kiss someone your heart beats faster and more oxygen reaches your brain. And it makes your pupils dilate.

- Our Lips are Hardwired to Fire Up the Brain and Parts of Our Body.

- Compulsive Kissing Syndrome Exists.

- Women tend to rate kissing as more important in relationships than men do.

- One French kiss requires 146 muscles to coordinate, including 34 facial muscles and 112 postural muscles.

- Our Love of kissing comes from ... Rats? The University of Tokyo believe that our affinity for kisses descends from an ancient rat. Mice and men have a surprisingly similar genetic makeup - sharing a common ancestor that lived sometime between 75 and 125 million years ago.

- According to anthropologists, 90 percent of people kiss. But that doesn't mean that kissing is the same for everyone. Kissing customs vary across the world.

- Kissing someone is more sanitary than shaking hands, if you want to avoid a cold.

- Philematology is the science of kissing. The scientific term for French kissing is cataglottism.

- In Nevada, it is illegal to kiss with a mustache.

- The average age in the UK for a first kiss is 15. Fewer than half the world's cultures engage in romantic kissing, a study found.

- The word "kiss" comes from the Old English word cyssan, which technically means "to kiss." No one is completely positive where cyssan comes from, but people suspect that it represented the sound people make when they kiss.

- At roughly 18 million years old, Mangaia Island is the oldest island in the Pacific Ocean. Despite all the time its inhabitants have had, they'd never heard of kissing until the English introduced them to the practice in the 1700s.

- Many Animals Other Than Humans Kiss. Even though it might not be exactly how we do it, several other animals engage in affectionate behavior that's remarkably similar to our kissing. Chimpanzees oftentimes demonstrate kiss-like behavior after a fight as a way to "kiss and make up" so to speak.

- Crazy as it may sound in 2014, there are still many countries where public affection is illegal. In Mexico, university professor Manuel Berumen was arrested for kissing his wife in public. In some countries, though, the punishments are extremely brutal. In 2010, a Saudi Arabian man was arrested for hugging and kissing a woman. He was found guilty and sentenced to three sets of 30 lashes each, plus four months in prison. Public kissing is also a crime in Indonesia punishable by five years in prison. Something to think about if you are visiting Bali.

- In Europe, it is proper etiquette to greet friends and family by kissing them on both cheeks.

- According to Guinness records, the longest documented kiss lasted 50 hours and 25 minutes by a Thai couple at an event that organized by Ripley's Believe It or Not! in Thailand, 2012.

- French Kissers Caused Commuter Headaches. Oh, the French. Apparently, in the early 20th century, so many French commuters were getting frisky on the train that they had to ban kissing, altogether.

- Kissing can increase your life expectancy. Men Who Kiss Their Wives Every Morning Live Longer.

- The average woman kisses 29 men before she gets married.

- As a rule, 66 percent of people keep their eyes closed while kissing. The rest take pleasure in watching the emotions run the gamut on the faces of their partners.

- Like fingerprints or snowflakes, no two lip impressions are alike.

- The longest kiss in movie history was between Jane Wyman and Regis Tommey in the 1941 film, You're in the Army Now. It lasted 3 minutes and

5 seconds. So, if you've beaten that record, it's time to celebrate!

- Dogs are the most kissable pet. I'm guessing that doesn't mean on the mouth. Or I am hoping.

- Kissing alleviates headaches and cramps.

- Forty-three percent of people would rather kiss their pet than their friends or family.

- Some women give off a scent when they are ovulating that is picked up by men when they are kissing. It could be subconscious, but it turns men on.

- Ever wonder how an "X" came to represent a kiss? Starting in the Middle Ages, people who could not read used an X as a signature. They would kiss this mark as a sign of sincerity. Eventually, the X came to represent the kiss itself.

- After a long hard day at work, many people experience back pain. Surprisingly, you should opt for kissing as opposed to pain relievers for treatment. As mentioned earlier, kissing releases endorphins in your body, which have been discovered to be more powerful than narcotics, such as morphine, when it comes to relieving pain.

- In China and Japan kissing is considered to be a private activity.

- Ancient Egyptians kissed with their noses. So did the Eskimos and Asian Pacific cultures—that's why rubbing noses is called an Eskimo Kiss.

Some cultures in the Himalayas don't kiss at all. Some cultures in Africa who don't kiss on the mouth because the mouth leads to the soul and someone who kisses you can take your soul. Butterfly kisses use only your eyelashes.

❖ At a study conducted at Butler University, John Butler asked some 500 people to discuss their most important memories. First kisses were the most vividly described memory, beating every other memory.

❖ Couples transfer an average of 9 milligrams of water, 0.7 milligrams of protein, 0.18 milligrams of organic matter, 0.71 milligrams of fat and 0.45 milligrams of salt to each other with each open-mouthed kiss

❖ Kissing can actually be a beauty treatment. Scientific tests show that good kissing helps reduce dermatitis, skin rashes and blemishes. It also makes your skin glow and your eyes shine. Kissing can help keep our facial muscles smooth and tight and even help prevent cheeks from sagging. If you want to keep that youthful glow you've got going, shower your love with kisses! Did anybody else just try the kissing motions to firm up their jowls or just me again?

❖ In Italy, kissing seems to be the social norm. Where in most of the world, about 56 percent of people report that they kiss passionately, 75 percent of Italians do! So, grab your passport and get ready to pucker up!

- The Oxford English Dictionary lists 52 words meaning a kiss or kissing.

- Kissing Regularly Can Help Resist Cheating. Scientists suspect that one of the culprits behind individuals cheating on their partners is a chemical called 'dopamine' which oozes throughout the body while kissing.

- France has a Kiss Map.

- When you kiss someone for the first time, you get a spike in the neurotransmitter dopamine, making you crave more. Dopamine can also make you lose your appetite and make it hard for you to sleep.

- Kissing helps us work out if someone is a good match. According to biological anthropologist Helen Fisher, we tend to prefer people with particular biological profiles. Trading saliva is one way to figure out if someone is a good fit.

- When you kiss someone your heart beats faster and more oxygen reaches your brain. All thanks to neurotransmitters epinephrine and norepinephrine which promote the fight-or-flight response. And it makes your pupils dilate. Which might be why we usually close our eyes.

- Endorphins released during kissing bring on waves of euphoria. You can thank your pituitary gland and hypothalamus for this natural high.

- Nachküssen is a German word that means "a kiss to make up for those that have not occurred".

- ❖ Kissing triggers the release of oxytocin in your body. Often called the "love hormone", though that's not all it does by a long stretch, oxytocin is involved in developing feelings of attachment. It's thought to be what keeps the love in a relationship alive long after the initial honeymoon period (and dopamine spike) is over.

- ❖ Women tend to rate kissing as more important in relationships than men do. The study, involving more than 1000 college students, also found that whereas women tend to use kissing to assess potential mates, men use it to increase the likelihood of sex.

- ❖ When your lips touch someone else's five out of twelve of your cranial nerves are engaged. Your brain is basically trying to gather as much information as it can about the other person.

2.
Take It in The Mouth

The sacrifices we make, getting spat in the eye, lock jaw, puking, gagged and yet we still love it.

BUMP THE BACK OF THE THROAT

- ❖ Fellatio is the technical term used to describe oral contact with the penis. And the word comes from the Latin verb fellāre, meaning "to suck."

- ❖ Cunnilingus describes oral contact with the clitoris, vulva, or vaginal opening. That word comes from the Neo-Latin words for the vulva (cunnus—which is also where the word cunt comes from!) and tongue (lingua). I would prefer you not to use these words while sexting. I would like to put my dick in your vaginal opening...

- ❖ Every time they engage in oral sex with their partner, 30 percent of women swallow.

- ❖ Anilingus refers to oral contact with the anus. And I imagine the term comes from the combination of anus and tongue. Because yes, eating ass needs a technical, science-y term. Obviously. TBH, how many people have really had their salad tossed? Or am I missing out?

- ❖ Over 80 percent of sexually active people ages 15-44 say that've had oral sex at least once with a partner of the opposite sex. And the other 20 percent just want to skip the gourmet meal and go straight for the dessert.

- ❖ "Blow job" came from the word "blowsy," which was slang for a prostitute. The word blow during the same period was slang for ejaculation. So, we're basically prostitutes who have a job to do. Cool.

- ❖ In ancient Greece, it was known as playing the flute. When I think of sucking cock, I think of the sound of sweet fluttering music.

- ❖ Bats give oral too. I fascinated to know how. Wolves and bears are also known to participate in the practice quite often.

- ❖ But humans are the only species creative enough to 69. Speaking of "69," the term was first seen in France during the 1790s. And the term was created by a lady named Theroigne de Mericourt. She was also known for writing a series of books called "Whore's Catechisms," and showing up to meetings of parliament for the sole purpose of heckling people. She also refused to wear clothes. So, like, she gets it.

- ❖ The HIV transmission risk for oral sex is significantly lower than it is for vaginal (and anal) counterparts. Like your drunk aunt always said, "Oral sex is safe sex."

- Foods such as kiwi, celery, and pineapple can make genital secretion sweet. Have people tried this? I would like to know if it actually works.

- Dairy products, meat, and alcohol are generally thought to worsen the taste. Like how though?

- Women who went to college are more likely to enjoy receiving and giving oral sex. I went to college and I'm going go with false, unless the dude knows what he is doing. Otherwise, I am bored.

- Think twice before swallowing if you're on a diet. There are five calories in a teaspoon of semen. Another report said 25 calories, but there is also .5g of protein in each serving☺ I also read another report that men who are vegetarians have sweeter tasting cum.

- Only one man in 400 is flexible enough to give himself oral sex. How many guys have tried though? Like all?

- A guy will ejaculate an average of 7,200 times during his lifetime. And the average number of times he'll ejaculate from masturbation is 2,000.

- The average speed of semen exiting his dong is 28 miles per hour. In case you want to try to outrun it before it splooges on you.

- ❖ No one knows how many women ejaculate during oral because most scientists think that the female orgasm is a myth. Okay, maybe not scientists. But definitely most guys between the ages of 18-106.

- ❖ Approximately 30 percent of women have orgasms from vaginal intercourse. Just remember, boys: When in doubt, get your tongue out.

- ❖ Only 55 percent of men ages 20-24 say that they've given oral in the past year. What in the actual fuck is the other 45 percent of them doing? Not giving orgasm, I can sure as shit tell you that.

- ❖ Whereas 74 percent of women ages 20-24 have given oral in the past year. I am not ok with this number.

- ❖ Oral sex during pregnancy is safe. However, you shouldn't blow air into the vagina during oral. It may cause an air embolism-air bubble trapped in a blood vessel-which can be harmful to the baby. Umm…if you blow air up my vagina, there is no way that is your baby.

- ❖ There are cave drawings of women giving men deep throat.

- ❖ In an old myth, the Egyptian god, Osiris, is hacked up to death but is reassembled by his faithful wife, who "blows life" back into him through his reconstructed penis. Speaking of Osiris, his father, the Earth god Geb, made appearances sucking his own penis because, apparently, it's a superpower.

❖ It's illegal to give blow jobs in Malaysia.

❖ Your lips become plump and kissable when you go down on someone. For how long though? It my save me some money.

❖ Sixty percent of women prefer to give blow jobs over hand jobs. Wait…aren't you supposed to use both?

❖ A hundred percent of guys prefer blow jobs to no blow jobs. No shit sherlock…

❖ In Ancient Rome men of status could receive, not give. It was common practice in Roman times that noble men and soldiers were on the receiving end of the BJ, while slaves and lower-class women would be the ones on their knees.

❖ In some cultures, drinking sperm is said to impart virility. In multiple cultures ingesting semen is a ritualistic act. In fact, the Chinese refer to it as "yang essence," and to achieve enlightenment it should never be wasted. Ancient Chinese sex manuals, in fact, depict various ways men would transfer their semen from their "heavenly dragon pillars" to their brains. Even in modern times, there are tribes like the Sambia of Papua New Guinea who require young men to perform fellatio and ingest semen in order to crossover into adulthood. Umm…no thank you.

❖ In ancient India sucking a mango, not a banana, represented the BJ. There is a chapter called "Auparishtaka," AKA "oral congress," in the *Kama Sutra* which gives a step by step guide for sucking the Johnson (an act considered to bring the giver good karma). Don't tell men though.

- ❖ As most of us know, any sex that is not for procreation purposes, according to many religions, is taboo. In the 19th century, it was announced that those who practiced onanism aka fellatio, petting, lesbianism, or masturbation would receive dire consequences, including caning and whipping. The influence of the religious stance against oral sex can still be seen in modern day, as veils serve in part to maintain the mouth's purity.

- ❖ Cleopatra may have serviced many, many men at once. Legend has it that the storied Egyptian queen blew more than 100 Roman noblemen during a marathon orgy. She was given the nickname "Meriochane," which translates to something like "someone who gapes for 10,000 men" in today's verbiage.

- ❖ Blow jobs were once given as criminal punishment. In Roman times punishment for breaking the law could be going down on the person you wronged. In fact, in the ruins of Pompeii, archaeologists uncovered graffiti that reads "Lahis fellat assibus duobus," which translates as "Lahis gives head for half a sentence."

- ❖ Ancient Peruvians decorated pots with all kinds of sexual hijinks. Turns out there was a civilization that existed between 100 to 800 A.D.

(before the Incas) in Peru who created tens of thousands of ceramics, covered in sexual acts. These dirty objects featured people, deities, skeletons, or animals in compromising positions, as well as plenty of oral and plenty of random phalluses.

- ❖ These sex pots have been found mostly in high-status burials, and were often accompanied by other religious artifacts, thus are believed to have been used in rituals. If you Google "Moche Sex Pots" you will not be disappointed.

- ❖ "Frenching" doesn't mean kissing, it means, well, you know…In the Renaissance, "Frenching" became shorthand for any type of genital kiss. It seems, at least according to a survey completed by Playboy, that the French have the upper hand on receiving oral, as they reported getting the most, followed Greeks, Brazilians, and Poles. This term is still used in modern day slang. Vive la France!

- ❖ While historians can't pinpoint the first blowjob ever, we know now that even Neolithic humans weren't afraid to go downtown. How do we know this? Because there are cave drawings depicting women giving men oral sex. In fact, there's even a cave portrait showing the story of a girl getting the Eiffel Tower.

- ❖ Even the most religious bible-thumpers can't hate on blowjobs, since they're mentioned in The Bible. Here's an excerpt from Songs of Solomon, Chapter 2, Verse 3: "Like an apple tree among the trees of the forest, so is my beloved among the young men. In his shade I took great delight and sat down, and his fruit was sweet to my taste."

- ❖ Bats are the only other organisms that practice fellatio. Female bats will often over and lick their partner's parts to extend intercourse. You'd think that the males would finish even faster, but that's strangely not the case. In instances where the female didn't lick her partner, the sex lasted an average of 100 seconds faster.

- ❖ An act of group sex restricted to one woman giving oral sex to several men is referred to as a gang-suck, blowbang or lineup, all derivatives of the slang term gang bang for group sex. Bukkake and gokkun may also involve oral sex.

- ❖ Opposite these views, people also believe that oral sex "is one of the most intimate behaviors that a couple can engage in because it requires total trust and vulnerability."

- ❖ A blowjob is the number one sexual act desired by straight men. Ugh. I'll suck it up if I have to. We need to make men want us, but they need to start treating us better because we could bite off their fucking dick if we wanted to. There is me getting angry, again. Ignore that. I love giving blow jobs.

3. Don't Be Silly, Protect Your Willie

JUST THE TIP

- ❖ What you see is only half of what you've got. Unfortunately, half of men's penis is tucked away inside their body and attached to the pubic bone.

- ❖ Your penis is crawling with bacteria. Researchers in Arizona found 42 types of bacteria on men's penises. I really don't care, most bacteria are…whatever.

- ❖ It takes over four ounces of blood to achieve an erection. One would assume that blood comes straight from the brain.

- ❖ Penis size is not correlated to shoe size.

- ❖ Penises stop growing in your early 20s. In other words, your penis stops growing right when you start growing up.

- ❖ Eighty percent of men living in the USA have been circumcised. And I've slept with most of them. The other 20 percent look like anteaters.

- A man's penis is never bigger than when he's receiving oral sex. A scientific study determined that men's penises measure the largest during a right good blowjob.

- Smoking can make your penis smaller. Enough said.

- Four-fifths of men are "growers"; the rest are "showers." Most men's penises grow much larger when they get an erection. The rest really don't improve much in size at all. Sucks to be them.

- Bigger penises may be an evolutionary advantage. This is because longer penises are better able to flush out a rival's sperm. That only happens in college.

- Only six percent of men require an extra-large condom according to condom manufactures. Although probably half of them buy them anyway. (More than half.)

- Penises are usually darker than the rest of your body.

- If you don't use it, you might lose it. Inactivity can shrink the penis from 1-2 centimeters. Well thank God for masturbation.

- With nothing in its path, a penis can shoot semen anywhere from 12 to 24 inches. Please don't try this at home.

- The underside is the most sensitive part. Are you taking notes, ladies?

- Globally, less than a third of men are circumcised. Although nearly two-thirds of American men are circumcised.

- Most men think they're smaller than they actually are. Even though they might brag that they're bigger than they actually are.

- Fetuses can have erections.

- It is almost impossible to achieve an erection in outer space. This is according to astronauts' personal testimonials.

- Some men have two penises. About 100 men in the world, to be exact. The condition is known as "diphallus." So, what does that look like.

- Hanging victims often achieve erections. But the "being dead" part makes it impossible to enjoy them.

- The smallest human penis ever recorded was 5/8 of an inch.

- The smallest animal penis is 1/5 of an inch. And it belongs to the male shrew. So, tell me again why they need to be tamed?

- The penis has no muscles. Instead, it's more like a sponge, except sponges aren't nearly as pleasurable.

- During missionary position, penises assume a boomerang shape. MRI evidence confirms this.

- The average male orgasm lasts 6 seconds.

- The most common cause of penile rupture: vigorous masturbation.

- Every year on average of 200 men break their penis.

- The largest penis is 13.5 inches long. I just threw up in my mouth…

- Men in The Republic of Congo are reported to have the largest penises.

- There is a museum in Iceland dedicated to the penis

- In Japan every year there is a festival devoted to celebrating the penis.

- Men in North Dakota reportedly buy the largest condoms in the U.S. While men in Mississippi buy the smallest ones.

- The male G-Spot is located on their prostate, while the perineum—the skin located in between the anus and the scrotum—is another major erogenous zone. Noted.

- The blue whale has the largest penis of any animal.

- In a condition called Diphallus, males are born with two penises. Only one fully works and it impacts 100 men worldwide.

- The adult male elephant has the largest penis of any land animal at six feet on average. It is S-shaped when fully erect.

- North and South Korea has the smallest ranked average penis.

- An estimated that 600 men will go to the ER for sex toy injuries in a year.

- Having sex at least once a week can lower a man's risk of heart disease by 30 percent, stroke by 50 percent, and diabetes by 40 percent.

- A man has an average of 11 erections per day. Nine of which are at night.

- About 30 million Americans struggle with erectile dysfunction.

- A "micropenis" is smaller than 2.8 inches in length when stretched.

- The penis stops growing when a man is in his early 20s.

- Shoe size does not determine penis size.

- Germany gets the most penis enlargement procedures in the world.

- There are two correct ways to mention multiple "members" in a sentence. The plural form of "penis" is "penises" or "penes".

- A man's penis will lose sensitivity with age. Studies have shown that the sensitivity of the male lance of love starts to decline at age 25.

- Doctors can use the foreskin of infants to grow skin grafts for burn victims. Supposedly one infant foreskin can produce 23,000 square meters of new skin. That's enough to cover every single major league infield.

- ❖ The reason one testicle hangs lower than the other is not because of size or weight, but so they don't smack into one another. If they were right in line with each other, men would have a serious problem trying to run.

- ❖ According to the *Penguin Atlas of Sexual Behavior*, there are over 166,666,000 people having sex every single minute, each day, around the world. This seems like a very possible alternative energy source if you ask me, with a pretty awesome incentive to help the world!

- ❖ Attractive men actually have stronger sperm. A study in Spain involved women ranking men based on their looks. The men that were found to be the best looking were most often the best sperm donors.

- ❖ A man who is recently deceased can actually pop a boner. This gives a whole new meaning to "Die Hard". Makes you think, doesn't it?

- ❖ King Louis XVI helped make circumcision popular because he suffered from phimosis. (I had to Google it too.)

- ❖ Within 24 hours, the average male experiences 11 erections. These things have a mind of their own.

- ❖ For men under the age of 40, their average time to erection is a mere ten seconds. For some it is shorter, and if it is much longer than ten seconds, it may be an indication of erectile dysfunction.

- ❖ The initial spurt of a man's ejaculation travels at approximately 28 miles per hour. I'm actually really disappointed with this fact. I always thought it was much faster.

- ❖ During an average man's lifetime, he will ejaculate approximately 17 liters of semen, which amounts to about half a trillion sperm.

- ❖ The testes increase in size by 50 percent when a man is sexually aroused.

- ❖ Over 30 percent of men suffer from premature ejaculation. 10% of men are affected by erectile dysfunction.

- ❖ The longer a man's ring finger is compared to his index finger, the more testosterone he has. Evidence also exists indicating that penis size may be linked to index finger length.

- ❖ Straight men tend to have smaller penises than gay men. Fuck, that sucks…

- ❖ Alfred Kinsey, author of Sexual Behavior in the Human Male (1948), had a collection of 5 million wasps and could insert a toothbrush into his penis, bristle-end first. Ok, he was not right in the head.

- ❖ Penises used to have spines Luckily, spiny penises evolved out before Neanderthals and modern humans diverged. Scientists are still not quite certain of the purpose of the spines.

Sarah Melland
HISTORY OF THE GLOVE

11,000 B.C.: Caves in France known as Grotte des Combarrelles are said to be the oldest evidence of condoms, with a painting on the wall that scientists say represents them.

1350 B.C.: Some historians argue that condoms made from cloth were used in ancient Egypt to protect against disease. They reportedly used condoms, probably made from animal bladders or intestines.

1400s A.D.: Glans condoms—ones that only covered the head of the penis—were used in China and Japan. In China, they were made from lamb intestines or oiled silk paper; in Japan, the materials of choice were tortoise shell or animal horn. Wasn't that hard? Ba-Dum-Tss…

1564: Italian physician and atomist Gabriele Fallopius recommended the use of a protective linen sheath, soaked in chemicals and dried, which would help prevent syphilis. Fallopius conducted an experiment using 1,100 participants to determine the early condom's effectiveness. None became infected with syphilis, but that sounds like sand paper.

1605: Catholic theologian Leonardus Lessius claimed in De Justitia et Jure that condoms are immoral. He was just pissed because he can't have sex.

1600s: Condoms made from animal intestines were first made available to the public. Because of their expensive nature, though, they were frequently reused. ~~That's~~ honestly so gross, I just can't. Please put that used cum infested thing back into my vagina, where my old juices have now crusted over.

1666: When the birth rate dropped, the English Birth Rate Commission attributed it to "condoms"—the first time that word had been published.

1700s: Condoms were fashioned from sheep, lamb and goat intestines, and sometimes fish skin. Can I just say how gross I think this is, not just for the male but for a female to have animal intestines in her vagina? Is that how STDs started? There has to be some weird fact about this. Did they still have the blood on the intestines?

1839: Charles Goodyear created rubber condoms.

1889: Ireland made it illegal to advertise condoms, though they could still be made and sold.

Late 1800s: People began using the term "rubber" to mean "condom."

1912: Julius Fromm, a German chemist, created a new means by which to manufacture condoms wherein he dipped glass molds into raw rubber solution, thus allowing them to have a texture. His line of condoms — Fromm's Act — remains popular in Germany today.

1918: A judge ruled that condoms can be advertised and sold to prevent diseases from spreading.

1920s: Condom companies stepped up their advertising by making packaging more interesting and names more intriguing. Sales of condoms doubled throughout the world in this decade.

1927-31: Condoms were often distributed to members of the American military and became standard issue for military men.

1950s and 1960s: Forty-two percent of Americans rely on condoms for birth control and STD prevention at this point in time.

1957: Durex reveals the first condom with lubrication.

1980s: In the face of the terrifying AIDS epidemic, the contraceptive is marketed as a way to prevent acquiring HIV. Condom use rose as a result.

1997: Durex created the first condom company website. Where is Trojan in all this? I am kind of disappointed Trojan Man.

2013: We now have the ability to buy condoms in all sorts of colors, flavors, textures and materials!

CONDOMS, CONDOMS EVERYWHERE WE'RE GONNA HAVE FUN

- ❖ The average condom can hold as much as 4 quarts of liquid—that's about a gallon, in case you were wondering.

- ❖ Condoms have flavors including bacon. I really don't know why you'd want to suck on them though.

- ❖ Proper condom use may seem like a no-brainer, but there are actually a lot of people out there that are really unsure or confused as to how to properly use a condom. The phrase "can you reuse a condom" produces more than 130,000 results on Google. In fact, the number one reason for contraceptive failure is USER ERROR.

❖ In 2003, the Guilin Latex Company made the world's largest condom. The condom was 260 feet tall and 330 feet around. It was erected on World Population Day in southern China. The Guilin Latex Co inflated the huge prophylactic with its 330-foot girth over the Fragrant River Hotel.

❖ In 2005 The obelisk in downtown Buenos Aires was covered by a giant pink condom as the city marked World AIDS Day. The city's health secretary said the condom was placed on the monument to show that "you cannot lower your guard" against AIDS.

❖ Brazilian artist Adriana Bertini made sculpture of condom, and clothing it by condoms. Adriana Bertini also created beautiful dresses from quality-test rejected condoms. Inspired by the HIV-positive children she got to know while volunteering for an AIDS prevention group,

❖ The origin of the word 'condom' is uncertain, but folklore attributes the invention to Dr. Condom or Conton, who was at the court of King Charles II in the 1600s. Or it could also be that the name derives from the Latin 'condus', meaning receptacle.

❖ The "Cho-San Express," is a truck that goes around the city, and for less than $10), you get 10 condoms delivered to the convenience of your home!

- ❖ Olympic Village Sex Festival. In the report, the *ESPN* writer revealed some rather scandalous facts, including that 100,000 condoms are ordered for the games. Apparently, officials at the 2000 Sydney Games had to put in an order for 20,000 extra condoms after the initial 70,000 ran out. Since then, an order of 100,000 has become the norm. In 2012, Durex provided over 150,000 condoms to athletes at the London Olympics, approximately 15 each. I mean the Olympic games are long…so it's not really that many.

- ❖ The word scumbag, by today's standards seems like a pretty mild insult to bestow upon someone who has crossed you. As it turns out, it's a pretty graphic, disgusting and super insulting word to have in your repertoire.

- ❖ The campus at Harvard has always been a wonderful place filled with the brightest minds conceptualizing the most forward thinking of ideas. Some Harvard students actually started a condom delivery service. They finally decided on the slogan "We'll Come Before You Do!"

- ❖ Magnum condoms are only .32 inches longer than regular ones.

- ❖ Don't worry, lambskin condoms aren't made from lambs' skin. They're made from their intestines!

- ❖ Among single people, one in three acts of vaginal intercourse involve a condom.

- Only 39 percent of high school students are taught how to properly put on a condom.

- Female condoms can be inserted up to eight hours before sex.

- September 16 is Global Female Condom Day.

- Condoms are strictly regulated by the FDA, just like Advil.

- All condoms undergo rigorous testing including water and air inflation tests as well as an electronic hole inspection. The robots keep your condoms safe.

- Get psyched, vegans—you can buy condoms that are completely animal byproduct free! I, on the other hand, will always wonder if vegans are allowed to swallow.

- Over 30 million free "NYC Condoms" are given out to New Yorkers every year...28 million of them to Derek Jeter.

- While in World War I, the U.S. and Britain were the only countries in the European conflict that didn't provide troops with condoms. They recorded over 400,000 cases of syphilis and gonorrhea.

- World War II marked the first war in which condoms were given to American troops.

- Zac Efron's mom once bought him condoms for Christmas.

- The first condom commercial burst onto the scene November 17, 1991, during an airing of "Herman's Head." How fitting…

- A condom company executive told ABC News that five billion condoms are sold annually to people all over the globe.

- While everybody knows about Magnum condoms, there are also condoms made for the undersized. NO one would ever admit to that though.

- The Guinness World Record for thinnest latex condom was set by Guangzhou Daming United Rubber Products Ltd. in 2013. The condom was .036 mm thin, which is very thin.

- In 2013 Bill and Melinda Gates received 812 entries in their "Build a Better Condom" competition. The 11 finalists received $100,000 each to make their wildest condom dreams come true.

- The average condom user is between 18 and 24 years old.

- Women worldwide purchase 40-70 percent of condoms.

- About 99 percent of condoms are made of latex. The rest are made from lamb intestines. Better known as Lamb skin? Glad to see we are still using animal intestines.

❖ In the 16th century condoms were made of linen. A ribbon sewn into the open end drew the condom snugly around the penis. Not going to lie that really sounds like it sucks for a dude. And I am hoping there was a lot of lube for females.

❖ Documentation suggests that legendary 19th century lover Casanova was a regular user of condoms, referring to them as 'redingote Anglaise' (English: riding coat).

❖ The Danish word for condom is Svangerskabsforebyggendemiddel. I've had blow jobs shorter. Probably…only because I got bored.

❖ The average shelf life of a latex condom is about two years. I did not know they had expiration dates, and discovered that I had to throw them away… It's like wasting alcohol, it should be a sin.

❖ It's a good idea to keep your own condoms since you don't know how long your partner's been holding on to his. Condoms kept in wallets for over a month are more likely to break. I feel like that should be a known fact, and if he is dumb enough to keep a condom in his wallet, please leave.

❖ Condoms don't actually make sex worse or less pleasurable. Straight women are just as likely to report having orgasms when their partner uses a condom as when he goes without. Yeah, I've never noticed a difference.

4.
Why Say Lubricant When You Can Say LubriCAN

IT'S LIKE A SLIP AND SLIDE DOWN THERE

People have used sexual lubricants for hundreds of years. There's a great deal of fascinating research showing how sexual aids developed along with various civilizations, and if you've ever wondered what ancient people used for personal lube, there are a few interesting answers.

The most common and obvious lubes are vegetable oils, which often played dozens of roles in growing agricultural societies. Early Greeks used olive oil for just about everything, including lubrication; the first written references to olive oil as a sexual lubricant date back to 350 B.C.

In one of his writings, the Greek philosopher Aristotle references the contraceptive powers of olive oil mixed with cedar oil, lead, and frankincense. From Greek texts, we also know that women would also use leather dildos lubricated with olive oil, and it stands to reason that olive oil was probably the go-to lubricant for that time period.

The Romans also used olive oil for sex and masturbation, and like the Greeks, they tried to incorporate contraceptives into their formulas. Pliny, the great Roman thinker, suggested a mixture of olive oil, pigeon droppings, and wine. Olive oil kept its popularity through the 16th century, which, incidentally, is around the time when the word "dildo" entered our vocabulary.

In Japan's Edo period (1603-1868), couples used tororo-jiru, a slick substance made by grating Chinese yams. Early Chinese condoms made from animal intestine or treated linen were often coated with a few drops of vegetable oil to facilitate penetration.

In the 19th century, gynecologists prescribed pelvic massages to women who couldn't produce enough natural lubrication. The physician would massage the woman's clitoris until she had an orgasm, at which point she was pronounced cured. These massages were also the go-to treatment for women who suffered from "excessive" lubrication, which is something of a testament to the repressive atmosphere of the time period.

K-Y Jelly was introduced in 1904 as a surgical product, and it is considered one of the first modern lubricants, as it uses a base consisting of methyl cellulose and other ingredients commonly found in newer water-based products. While it was not marketed for sexual use, its manufacturer began offering a non-sterile version for non-surgical use.

The sexual revolution of the 1960s made lubricants and other products more socially acceptable, and manufacturers like K-Y quickly shopped their products to a new audience. The lubricant industry gained steam in the 1990s and 2000s, and the market now features hundreds of specially formulated products designed to please different types of users.

Modern lubricants are much safer than their forebears and much less likely to cause infections or to foster microorganism growth. We've certainly made major advances since the days of olive oil and tororo-jiru, and personal lubricants will continue to help people enjoy themselves in safe, new, and exciting ways for centuries to come.

Now we have passion parties and all that jazz. We have lubes that if we blow, they get warm and everything in between. Google passion parties and throw one for you and your girlfriends. It will be totally worth it.

TO LUBE, OR NOT TO LUBE, THAT IS THE QUESTION

- ❖ Water-based lubes are the most common type of lube. They're easy to wash off but dry quickly, meaning you'll need to reapply the lube a couple of times during longer sessions.

- ❖ Silicone-based lubes last longer than water-based lube. It also doesn't blend with water so they're good to use in the shower or other water environments.

- ❖ Silicone-based lubes are safe to use with condoms, they shouldn't be used with silicone sex toys as it will break down the material, which could let bacteria in.

- ❖ Silicone-based lubes can also be difficult to remove.

- ❖ Oil-based lubes, like Vaseline, are best used for hand jobs and unprotected sex, as this lube breaks down latex condoms. It can also be used for sexual activities that include bigger... equipment. For example, fisting.

- ❖ Powder-based lube comes in a powder form which needs to be mixed with water to create the lube. This means that you can make it as thick or as thin as you wish, depending on the activity you're going to use it for. That, also, just sounds like a mess. Hold on honey, let me mix the lube.

- ❖ Cream-based lubes are rarer and used mostly for anal play. It is designed to be used for sex with bigger objects, such as toys and fists. Every time I hear the word fist, I tense up.

- ❖ Lube has an expiry date. Once the bottle is opened, it's more likely to expire sooner, so it's best to use it within a year.

- ❖ You should always keep your lube at room temperature and with the bottle closed.

- ❖ Lube can help ease discomfort in women that have vaginal dryness.

- ❖ A well-lubricated penis enhances pleasure for the man, whether it be during sex or masturbation. It can also help sex last longer.

- ❖ Lubricants that cause tingling sensations or are dyed can give an allergic reaction.

- ❖ Lube can help sustain an erection for men that have trouble staying aroused.

- ❖ Lubricants can cause sperm motility problems, making it difficult for couples to conceive. There are sperm-friendly lubes that claim to counter this though.

- ❖ Using lube substitutions like Vaseline or baby oil can cause yeast infections, that can damage vaginal tissue. Also, don't use lubes that use glycerin.

- ❖ Saliva can be used in place of lube but as it's waterier, it dries out quicker. I hate when guys spit on their dick.

- ❖ Lube can help to prevent tissue damage for both men and women.

5.
I Want Your Sex, Baby

Here it is! The motherload of all mother loads, the beast with two backs, the whore and the pimp, the masterful making whoopee, and everything you have ever wanted to know about the crazy thing we like to do a lot.

- ❖ Average sex lasts 2 min and 50 seconds.

- ❖ Women are more willing to commit adultery during their ovulation than at any other time throughout their cycle—most notably due to their bodies' desire to fertilize the ovulated egg. I know I want a one-night stand with a random, when I want to get pregnant…

- ❖ Most women who lose their virginity between ages 15 and 19 actually wish they had waited a bit longer. Additionally, most teenagers lose their virginity by age 17, but those who have not lost their virginity by 24 tend to stay a virgin. I am guessing they will stay a virgin until they are married. Not for life. God that would be awful.

- ❖ If a female ferret does not have sex for a year, she will die. We should all be thanking God right now, that we are not ferrets. And for those of you who have female ferrets, you better get a male.

❖ During intercourse, your inner nose swells just as your breasts and genitals will. This is most notably due to the increased flow of blood while having intercourse. I always thought I could breathe easier while I was having sex. Except most of the time I'm holding it in.

❖ For men, sex burns between 100 and 200 calories on average. On the other hand, it only burns approximately 69 calories for women. I would beg to differ, but that's just personal opinion and is not based on fact.

❖ There is enough sperm in one single man to impregnate every woman on the planet who is fertile. Men – Are you ready for a challenge? I am just kidding, don't do that.

❖ Studies show that lower cholesterol is directly related to a better performance in the bedroom. Like I always said before sex, please get your cholesterol checked, it's important for your health, so you don't have a heart attack during intercourse.

❖ Approximately one third of women in their 80's continue to have sex with their husband or boyfriend. YES! YES! YES!

❖ While many know that chocolate can be an excellent arousal for having sex, apparently the smell of pumpkin can help increase the blood flow to the penis and encourage an erection.

❖ Low blood sugar can easily cause harm to your love life as low blood sugar makes you irritable and less likely to want your partner. Get me a damn chocolate chip cookie!!!!

- ❖ At the point of orgasm, both men and women tend to have a heart rate of approximately 140. This is not excessive, but just enters the common cardiovascular zone. That is the perfect fat burning zone...now only if he could last 20 minutes, it could be my workout.

- ❖ For those intrigued by having a threesome, you will need to travel to Australia as 28% of the population admits to having done a threesome at least once. Ummm... I am really curious as to why that is.

- ❖ Only five percent of the population have sex once a day, while 20 percent have sex 3-4 times a week. The rest of the population are unknown, but hopefully not too spread out. I would just like to say that leaves 75 percent unaccounted for. So ladies, that means guys are not having as much sex as they say they are. DO NOT be intimidated!

- ❖ Women have the ability to make their voice sound "sexier" in order to entice their men when needed. Men, however, do not possess such an ability and simply have to rely on other factors. Hahaha, I don't even know anymore. This is amazing.

- ❖ Approximately 60 percent of men who get aroused have erect nipples. In fact, the nipples are just as sensitive in men as they are in women, which is why so many men get erect nipples. Ladies, start paying attention to their nipples.

❖ In order to know how much testosterone a man has, compare the length of his ring finger to his index finger. The longer the ring finger is in comparison to the index finger, the more testosterone in his body. I don't understand about testosterone. Does that mean he's good in bed?

❖ For a woman attempting to reach climax, it will take her only four minutes through masturbation. However, it can take upwards of 10-20 minutes to reach climax during intercourse. I am at a solid minute, 30 seconds if I am really turned on or just woke up from a sex dream.

❖ Women who are prone to migraines are also more likely to have more sex, this is because orgasms can help alleviate the pain of a migraine. They also have a higher sex drive because of this issue. Sex can relieve a headache – it releases the tension, which restricts blood vessels in the brain. Goodbye Ibuprofen, hello sex!

❖ Approximately one percent of women can achieve full orgasm solely through stimulating their breasts. Anybody want to try this with me? What does a breast orgasm feel like?

❖ Nearly two thirds of all men and women have fantasized about another person while having sexual intercourse with their current partner. Typically, the one being fantasized about is not someone they will be able to have intercourse with. So, you're saying I won't be able to have sex with Channing Tatum? Damn…sad face emoji.

Yeah, I wrote it, who cares, you should know me by now.

- When you are aroused and prepped for sexual intercourse, you are actually less likely to be grossed out by anything that happens. That explains a lot.

- We automatically perceive people who smell good as more attractive. I feel like there is a "Duh" in there somewhere.

- Ginger stimulates the feelings of excitement associated with sex. Eating ginger elevates your heart rate, gets your blood flowing and gets you excited for the night ahead.

- A study found that men feel more emotional pain after a breakup than women do. I feel like that's a lie, who were their placebos? If they are, they have a weird way of showing it. And I have no idea how this relates sex, but while we are here, buy my other book, *The Breakup Band Aid.*

- Sperm can be considered an anti-aging treatment, as it has a tightening effect on the skin. I am only going to try this one time, and then I'm out.

- Sleep deprived men are more likely to believe that women want to have sex with them. This is not a joke.

- People who are into kinkier sex may be psychologically healthier. Shit… I guess bring out the damn beads.

- Endorphins released during sexual activity create a euphoria similar to opioid drug use.

- Some people experience the same feeling of arousal when thinking about food as when having sex. Totally get it.

- After ovulation, a female's egg is fertile for 24 to 48 hours and a man's sperm can live 48 hours in the female body. There have been documented cases of live sperm discovered eight days after sex. Another report I read said even up to nine days. So, don't let them spew in you unless you really, really want to get preggo.

- Twelve percent of adults have had sex at work. There is another report that said 15%, I really feel those numbers are low…

- Around 30 percent of women have trouble reaching orgasm. I said it once, but I will say it again, MEN, rub the damn Clitoris!

- A study found that good sex triggers the region of the brain associated with falling in love. No fucking wonder…

- According to a study, people who have sex once or twice a week have their immune systems boosted slightly.

- A man can reduce his chances of getting prostate cancer by having at least four orgasms a week. I wonder if this report includes masturbation. It must. I am a firm believer in masturbation. It is good for the soul.

❖ There are some foods that boost your sex drive, one of them being black raspberries. This phytochemical-rich food enhances both libido and endurance. Oysters are high in zinc, which is vital for testosterone production and healthy sperm. Watermelon contains citrulline amino acid, good for the cardiovascular system and helps relax the blood vessels that increase your sex drive.

❖ The average vagina is three to four inches long but can expand by 200 percent when sexually aroused. K, so I read this and am not so aligned to this statistic. Another report said four inches aroused, I am going to go with that one. I have had huge penises in me before and it hurts when they are too big. It is definitely not the most enjoyable. That's when women on top comes in handy. You can maneuver that shit so it doesn't go so deep it hits your fucking cervix.

❖ Sex is 10 times more effective than Valium.

❖ Shaving your pubic area increases your chances of spreading an STI. Sorry ladies, that also includes waxing because it can cause irritation and micro-trauma to your skin. Contrary to what the newbies of pubic hair might think it does have huge purposes. It helps prevent foreign particles like dust and pathogenic bacteria from entering your body, reduces friction, which prevents skin irritation, abrasion and injury. Promotes touch reception. The last one I think makes us more sensitive. I am just saying that because that's what it sounds like. I am not going to lie; I really am starting to like the look of pubic hair. Not, of course, outside my bikini area, but just nice and trimmed is kind of sexy. Also, this fact didn't say if laser hair removal would be ok, so I am not sure. Also, men don't give a fuck.

❖ Yes, they are now called STIs (sexually transmitted infections) instead of STDs (sexually transmitted diseases). I feel like STI's are the curable ones, and STDs are your herpes, genital warts etc. I am totally making that up and have no idea, but that's the only logical reason that makes sense.

❖ A woman's butt sticks out 25 percent more when she is wearing heels. They do look so amazing, but why do heels have to hurt so bad, will someone please make some insert for a shoe, so that they will never ever hurt...

❖ The nerve endings in the clitoris extend out to where the pubic hair grows, which is why grinding (dry humping) feels so good.

❖ Your pain threshold can increase significantly during arousal.

❖ You should pee as soon as possible after sex to prevent UTIs (urinary tract infections). Women you know this! Don't risk it. It's like in every issue of Cosmo to do this. Don't be stupid. UTIs are annoying and painful.

❖ Every year, 11,000 Americans injure themselves when trying out bizarre sexual positions. I, however, am not that adventurous and don't want to get a gerbil stuck up my ass and running through my intestines.

❖ The average sexual experience lasts 37 minutes. That has to include foreplay. Yes, I get my facts from the internet and no I don't check. If they are all the same on like eight internet sources it must be true. We aren't talking politics here.

❖ According to a survey of adults aged 20 to 59, women have an average of four sex partners during their lifetimes and men have an average of seven. Oops...

❖ Some sexual dysfunction can stem from how a woman feels about the appearance of her genitals. Again, men don't give a shit.

❖ Festival-goers would rather spend time doing drugs, drinking and having sex than watching the concert they paid big money to see. Oh, so that's what they do at Coachella?

❖ Women with higher testosterone levels might be more interested in masturbation than having sex with someone else. How do we know if we have higher testosterone levels? I masturbate a lot. Apparently, hair loss, acne, lower voice, coarse hair on chin and abdomen, diminished breasts, is how you tell. I guess that makes sense. Well...my chest is not going anywhere, so I figured out my answer.

❖ Nipples are erogenous zones because the sensation of hardened nipples travels to the same part of the brain as sensations from the vagina, cervix and the clitoris.

❖ At least 50 percent of sexually active people will have HPV at some point in their lives. According to the Centers for Disease Control and Prevention, in 90 percent of cases, the body's immune system will fight off the disease within two years. That I know is true. If you have HPV, every day take a multi-vitamin, Vitamin A, and Folic Acid, it will help get rid of it faster.

❖ About 75 percent of men always reach orgasm during sex and only 29 percent of women do. Actually, most women aren't able to climax through straight vaginal intercourse and need some clitoral stimulation to help them achieve orgasm. Women, AGAIN, stop faking your fucking orgasms.

❖ Telling a convincing lie to someone is much more difficult when you find them sexually attractive.

❖ Small quantities of over 30 different substances have been identified in human semen. These include nitrogen, fructose, lactic acid, ascorbic acid, inositol, cholesterol, glutathione, creatine, pyruvic acid, citric acid, sorbitol, urea, uric acid and Vitamin B12, along with various salts and enzymes.

❖ Chocolate contains phenylethylamine, the same feel-good chemical responsible for the ecstatic high people experience through sexual attraction and love.

- ❖ Women who have given birth have darker labia minora than women who haven't. So, what you're telling me is I am going to have darker inner lips after giving birth? I feel like that is the least of my worries.

- ❖ The majority of women experience a peak in libido just before their period.

- ❖ -321°F is the temperature at which sperm banks store donor semen. At this temperature, semen can be stored indefinitely. Does that mean they shrink? Ba-Dum-Tss.

- ❖ The point at which the average man reaches his sexual peak is between the ages of 17 and 18. That has to suck a little bit. While women peak in their mid-thirties. Don't fret boys, there are new studies that show men have the best sex at 32, women, however, are the most fertile around 26. I am going to come right out and say it, I am always at my sexual peak, and I just keep getting better.

- ❖ The earth could be re-populated to its current level using the number of sperm that could fit into an aspirin capsule. I know this is similar to the one above, but is it not crazy to think about? On average, from two to five million sperm are released each time a man ejaculates.

- ❖ A chicken egg could accommodate the number of female ova necessary to repopulate the earth to its present numbers. We better know this from health class or we are failing as a society.

- White women are the most likely to engage in anal sex, particularly if they also have a college degree. Ok. I really want to know who found that statistic.

- During erection, a smaller flaccid penis tends to have a greater percentage increase than a larger flaccid penis. I am going to go with duh, on this one. We have all heard the term grower not a shower.

- During any given period, women who read romance novels have a tendency to have twice as many lovers as those who don't. HAHA.

- The average woman will have sex more than 3,000 times over the course of her reproductive years. Fuck! I don't think I am that high at all, I better get moving.

- Heterosexual anal sex is something 43% of women have experienced. Hmm…I feel like that is high. I am going to do some more research. Where were these tests done? Utah, sounds about right. (Please for the love of God get that joke.)

- Women consider penis size the ninth most important feature for a man, while men rate it much more highly, in third place. Guys need to calm down. Or maybe they should think, we think that is number one so that stop being such assholes. The average penis size though is 5.6 inches, that is sufficient.

- In one hour, the average sperm can swim seven inches. So, you are telling me they are fast?

- There are 20 male masochists for every female masochist. Why does this statistic not surprise me?

- For 75 percent of men, ejaculation occurs within 3 minutes of penetration. FUCK! You better get me off asshole. That is so fast, that is the new meaning of minute man.

- One in 50 people claim to have had sex in an airplane. That sounds up there. That means about four people each plane ride made it in the mile-high club. I could see getting it on in a private jet. I would do that, but not in an airplane porta potty. There is barely enough room for you. Is one person over the toilet? I need to get more flexible.

- Forty-one percent of men would like to have sex more frequently. Only 29 percent of women share this urge. Are you sure this statistic isn't around 93 percent? Doesn't everyone want more sex, or is that just me? I mean I want good sex all the time, but bad sex seems to happen more frequently.

- Greek couples have sex an average of 138 times a year—placing them at the top of the world sex league. Japanese couples have sex just 45 times a year, which puts them in last place.

- Half of single women have sex by the third date. I'm a third date girl for sure unless it falls on a period cycle.

- Women over 40 years of age are more likely to masturbate than any other group. Are they single or married? I masturbate more than anyone I know, so I feel this statistic could be wrong. Yes, I even masturbate in relationships. Once I start, I need more, and I need it all the time.

❖ There's a direct link between how often a man has sex and his life expectancy. I am guessing they have a higher life expectancy, because they sure enjoyed it.

❖ Forty-four percent of women find it impossible to enjoy sex with a man who is not their intellectual equal. Just 31 percent of men share this problem.

❖ At any given time, 25 percent of people are daydreaming about sex. I make that number go way up. I think about having hot steamy sex all the time. That's why I write about it. It's fun☺

❖ Over half of American adults have used the phone, email or text message to have sex. I think it happened to me once, but I was not paying attention as I was checking my social media as he jacked off. I might have moaned to help, but I was bored. It wasn't someone I would ever have sex with so I guess phone would have to do.

❖ According to studies, the larger a man's testicles, the more likely he is to stray.

❖ Seventy-five percent of Japanese women own a vibrator. The average worldwide is 47 percent. This is the point I was just talking about. No one in Japan is having sex.

- During their lifetime, the average driver will have sex in their car six times. Six times? Shit…I haven't even had it once; I've made out in a car. I am boring.

- Americans spend twice as much money on pornography as they do on biscuits. Umm…who spends money on biscuits?

- One in five women living with their boyfriend has more than one sexual partner. I feel like most women will have more than one sexual partner in their lifetime.

- Besides humans, bonobos (a type of chimp) and dolphins are the only animals that have sex for pleasure.

- Eighty-five percent of women are very satisfied with their partner's penis size. The other 15% are dealing with centimeters.

- The number of wet dreams a man is likely to have increases in line with the number of years spent in formal education. When do men stop having wet dreams?

- Compared to anywhere else, adults are more likely to tell a lie in bed.

- The majority of women prefer to have sex in the dark. Ummm… Duh?

- Men find women with enlarged pupils more sexually attractive. Do they mean they find women more attractive when they are high? Or is it too dim of lighting?

- ❖ When having sex, black women are 50 percent more likely to reach orgasm than white women. I think they fake it.

- ❖ Sixty percent of non-smoking women have had no sexual partners in the past year, while 70% of women who smoke have had more than four lovers over the same timescale.

- ❖ Thirty-four percent of men have told lies in order to have sex. Ten percent of women have done the same. Men tell way more than they are admitting to, which is also a lie.

- ❖ More than 50 percent of all cheating wives choose married men as their lovers. Bitches always need to ruin everything.

- ❖ Within the week, 22 percent of women tell at least five friends about their first sexual experience with a partner. I tell way more, haha.

- ❖ Two-thirds of runners admit to having thought about sex while running. You can think about sex anytime, I don't know why this is a relevant fact.

- ❖ Sixty-eight percent of men and 59 percent of women had a sexual liaison with someone in their past, which they have not told their current partner about. I mean if you sleep with 20 people, do you really have to tell your partner about all of them? I don't even remember all their names; some were just by the city they were from.

❖ An overwhelming majority of sexual partners have only skimpy knowledge of what truly turns each other on. Why don't we talk to one another instead of being on our fucking phones the whole time?

❖ One in ten European babies is conceived in an IKEA bed. Who cares?

❖ British spies stopped using semen as invisible ink because it began to smell if it wasn't fresh. Wait, can we talk for a second on how they used semen as invisible ink?

❖ A single sperm contains 37.5 MB of DNA information. One ejaculation represents a data transfer of 15.875 TB, equivalent to the combined capacity of 62 MacBook Pro laptops. For all you techie nerds out there, this fact is for you.

❖ Male fruit flies rejected by females drink significantly more alcohol than those that have had a successful encounter. Haha, ok…

❖ Seven Viagra tablets are sold every second. So, you are saying I should buy stock in Viagra?

❖ The German word for "contraceptive" is Schwangerschaftsverhütungsmittel. Where is Heidi Klum when you need a pronunciation?

❖ The best-selling work of fiction of the 15th century was "The Tale of the Two Lovers," an erotic novel by the man who later became Pope Pius II. I would like to read this book. The End.

- In 2008, archaeologists in Cyprus found a 7th-century curse inscribed on a lead tablet that said, "May your penis hurt when you make love." Nobody knows who made the curse, or why. For sure, it was a woman.

- The founder of match.com, Gary Kremen, lost his girlfriend to a man she met on match.com. Oh, the irony...

- Gymnophoria is the sense that someone is mentally undressing you. I am gymnophoriaing you right now, Channing Tatum.

- A female chimpanzee in a fit of passion has the strength of six men.

- The "G-spot" was nearly called the Whipple Tickle- after Professor Beverley Whipple, who coined the expression we know today.

- Crocodile dung used to be used as contraception. Ancient Egyptian women used crocodile dung as contraception - dung is slightly alkaline, so it may have worked as a spermicide. Did it not smell? Or didn't they care?

- Each year in Brooklyn, there is the Smallest Penis in Brooklyn contest. Who would actually participate in these shenanigans?

- Studies have shown that men have less sex when they do more housework. Coincidentally, women won't have sex with men who don't do what they are told.

❖ Researchers found that overweight men lasted almost three times as long in the bedroom. I'm not going to make a joke here.

❖ Some studies suggest that men whose wives earn more money than them are more likely to experienced erectile dysfunction.

❖ About 33 percent of Americans get injured during sex. I like a good choking every now and then.

❖ This age-old controversy seems to be settled. Scientists have recently reported that some of the fluid in female ejaculate is pee, but the rest is just prostate fluid. I don't know how I feel about this. Prostate fluid? What the fuck is that?

❖ Apparently, semen contains chemicals that elevate mood, increase affection, and induce sleep, it also contains cortisol, which is known to increase feelings of affection in the brain. It also reduces the chance of breast cancer by 40 percent, I read that on CNN.

❖ The order to ejaculate comes from the spinal cord, not the brain.

❖ Seniors are kind of into oral. Thirty-seven percent of men and 25 percent of women 50-80+ gave oral sex in the past year, according to the Indiana University Journal of Sexual Medicine.

❖ Male septuagenarians have more sex. According to some studies, males over 70 have 230 times more sex than women over 70. This statistic breaks my heart.

- ❖ Artists and poets get laid more. Some studies have suggested that creative people have more sex. I would agree, except when I am being an introvert.

6. I Think It's Time We Talk About Sex Toys

I don't know why I decided to put this little gem in here. Take what you want and leave the rest. It's good to have knowledge.

35,000 BP – Pornography: Archaeologists uncovered a pervious prehistoric statue. Carved from mammoth tusk, it featured a female torso with exaggerated sexual parts. Although its age is uncertain, the best guess places it at over 35,000 years old; which means it may even pre-date religion.

30,000 BP: The first phallic sex devices were depicted in Paleolithic cave art dating as far back as 30,000 BP.

26,000 BP – The Dildo: The oldest known insertable tool was an 8 and a half inch stone phallus, unearthed in Hohle Fels Cave in Ulm Germany, that's during the Ice Age!

2000 BP: A brothel recently unearthed in Athens, Greece where a fully-stocked "sex toy" shop (stone vaginal and anal probes, penis paraphernalia, and a variety of lubricants) was discovered. According to numerous historic texts, sex tools—especially penis-shaped dildos—were so integral to day-to-day Grecian life that they were commonly sold in the marketplace, and men and women took them virtually everywhere they went—even into the afterlife.

100 A.D. – The Bible Comments: Because you were wondering, the Bible does not mention sex toys. Nor does it actually condemn masturbation. It does, however, denounce impurity and explicitly mentions thoughts about adultery.

300 A.D – Penis Extenders: Penis extender sleeves became commonly used in Asia. In the *Kama Sutra* and its companion, *The Hindu Art of Love*, penis extenders were advocated for men needing a longer penis (they say to satisfy women with larger vaginas—I'm going to just keep laughing) or to enable impotent men to please their wives like a modern-day strap-on. The *Kama Sutra* suggests wood, leather, ivory, gold, silver, copper, and even buffalo horns as good natural substances from which to carve them.

500 A.D – Geisha Balls: Japanese developed the Geisha Balls (also known as Ben Wa Balls, Rin No Tama or Burmese Balls). It was originally used to pleasure men. Initially a single, solid spherical orb inserted into the vagina before intercourse, they evolved into a pair of balls connected by a string, one solid, one hollow, which when inserted together bump into each other as the woman moves, and meant to be worn throughout the day to bring sustained sexual pleasure. These balls were crafted of silver, gold, jade, ivory, and numerous other substances--and have enjoyed a resurgence of popularity since rediscovered by the Baby-boomer generation of the 1960s. Ben Wa balls can be used to strengthen vaginal muscles, and women sometimes carry them around all day for that purpose. In earlier times, Ben Wa balls were often made of metal and sometimes rusted due to overuse. Modern-day versions, however, are generally coated with silicone for sterility reasons to prevent rust.

1200 A.D – Penis Ring: It was during the Jin and Song Dynasties of China that the penis or "cock" ring became a popular bedroom accessory across Asia. Documents from the period describe the first rings as being made from the eyelids of goats--with the lashes still intact. The eyelid rings are said to have been tied around a man's erection, with the hardened lashes intended to add additional stimulation for the woman during thrusting. By 400 BP, penis rings were being carved from ivory and were used primarily to help men maintain erections longer. Over the next few centuries, little nubs were added to the ring to act as clitoris stimulators. Penis rings later became status symbols throughout China, with wealthy and prominent men opting for rare and exotic materials to encircle and draw attention to their members. It wasn't easy being ancient Chinese nobility. If you didn't produce an heir, you could be pretty sure some obscure prince was going to step up. In such stressful circumstances, performing can become—well, difficult.

1500 A.D – Beautiful words: Poet Thomas Nashe wrote a piece, entitled "The Choice of Valentines or the Merie Ballad of Nash His Dildo." It is a heartwarming tale of a young boy's first sexual encounter, which takes place in a brothel with a hooker and a glass dildo. It is the first recorded use of the word, "dildo" in the English language.

1892 A.D – Butt Plugs: Frank E. Young had the vision of Butt plugs. Developed in 1892 but not marketed until the turn of the century. His 'Rectal Dilator' was a terrifying four and a half inches of pain. Billed as a cure for piles, the devices were hawked to doctors and even advertised in respected journals. People might well have gone on believing they were medical devices too, were it not for the ridiculously suggestive instruction manual. For 40 years these Victorian butt plugs were sold across the United States, before falling foul of the 1938 Federal Food, Drugs and Cosmetics Act, which banned them for "false advertising."

1904 A.D – Blow up Dolls: Lady substitutes are recorded as far back as the seventeenth century, when French sailors devised the Dame de Voyage: a collection of curvaceous rags that could only ever resemble a woman to a homesick Frenchman. But it wasn't until vulcanized rubber was patented that the more familiar model came about: in 1904, alchemist Rene Schwaeble. Less than four years later, German dermatologist Iwan Bloch was marveling over mass-manufactured versions that could 'imitate ejaculation' on sale in Parisian catalogues. Creepiest of all though has to be the firm offering a custom doll resembling "any actual person, living or dead"—which has to be the single most disturbing tagline in the history of advertising.

1983 A.D – Virtual Sex: Virtual sex has become a reality—even beyond that first introduced by the 1983 cyber-classic *Brainstorm*—with several reputable electronics companies now offering devices that can be attached to the penis or vagina for virtual sex through Internet connection. Researchers in England are even testing a computer chip that can be inserted under the skin to allow Internet connected individuals to link sexually-- the sexual thoughts of one sexually stimulating the other.

LET'S GET INTO THAT KINKY SHIT

Pig Tail Butt Plug. What is the need of the tail? Easy pull-out method? Can it do double duty? Easy grip method so it never gets lost in your anus?

Area 51 Love Doll. "It's pussy-shaped mouth, three supple breasts, suction cup fingers and ass-shaped ears make it the kinkiest love slave in the galaxy." I am at a loss for words. For all your big bang theorists out there.

Hooded Spandex Full Body Binder Sack. I feel like they invented this after seeing the first season of American Horror Story.

Rubber Gates of Hell. "Corral your stallion with these slightly stretchy rings designed to please and tease." What if their penis isn't long enough for these luscious rings?

Houdini Locking Steel Cock Chastity. "The tubular steel design makes it impossible to masturbate with this in place and the ratcheting cuff makes sure it stays put until the key master is in the mood to release you." If you have a son that masturbates too much, this device is for you…It also said it was around 10 pounds. It even has a cute little handcuff around it.

The Perfect Pair Breast Enhancers. Yes…Roger…I agree…strap on breast for men is going to be a revolution! Why didn't we think of this sooner? What the flying fuck?

The Cone. This was designed because of a stupid quote in Billy Madison… I am really glad it shows you various ways to use it.

Anal Speculum. "Perfect for medical/clinic scenes for the sadistic proctologist." Are we giving anal pap smears now? Oh, we are. Ok. Cool.

Orca. Yes, this is what an Orca's dick looks like. It is over 15 inches long and dishwasher safe.

The Hot Seat Inflatable Cushion Vibe. Oh my God yes! Now this is something I would actually buy. Clamp your legs to it and start hopping around your living room. I want one so bad. I am so turned on right now…excuse me for a moment.

Rubber Fisting Mitten. This also comes in a variety of different colors. It looks like a torpedo and scares me. The end. Big restriction on the box though: Use plenty of latex safe silicone lubricant when using this.

Electro-Sex Glove Set. Yes! Now I don't have to rub my socks on the carpet really fast to shock someone. Electrocution at its best. The jury is out on this one if you are being a bad boy.

The Tongue Vibrator. So, I took these from an article on some guy's website, and he thinks this will inspire a horror movie. I, however, am very intrigued and will probably be purchasing this. It has different speeds and looks like it goes in different directions. Just put a little coconut oil on that shit and you are good to go.

I Rub My Duckie Massager. "Just pop in the two AA batteries (included), flip the duckie on and utilize it till your heart's content." I don't know why I find this the creepiest one of all…maybe because it's a children's toy and something so pedophiliac about it.

Auto Suck. 'Do not use while driving!' Let me get this straight, it plugs into a car lighter, but should not be used while driving? I know I just like to go out to my car and masturbate there instead of in my bed.

Kaylani's Foot Fetish. Oh, look she's even wearing strappy sandals but wait...Is there a vagina on this foot? I don't know what to do anymore.

The Pleasure Periscope. Yay! Maybe he will finally find my G-spot...or just look at disgusting flesh.

Dildo Gas Mask. Hey, I have just the thing if we are going through the apocalypse.

Prince's Wand. Yes, it looks like your original vibrator, but it's actually supposed to be stuck up your pee hole. Please make it stop. Make it stop.

Mr. Jack with Mustache. This is meant for a guy who wants a blowjob from Burt Reynolds.

BONUS: I am not even joking, there is a new gadget called the selfie stick dildo, so you can take selfies while you masturbate, how convenient.

INTERESTING SEX TOY FACTS

- ❖ I will not be moving to Alabama as it is illegal to sell sex toys. According to the assistant attorney general in 1999, "there is no fundamental right for a person to buy a device to produce orgasm." Sex toys are also outlawed in India.

- During a LiveScience study in 2011, about half the subjects agreed with positive statements about the sex toys, while just 10 percent agreed with negative statements.
- According to that same study, 37 percent of women believed men felt intimidated by women's vibrator use, but 70 percent of men actually were totally fine with sex toys.
- Eighty-four percent of sex toy buyers use toys for clitoral orgasms, more than the 64 percent that use dildos or strap-ons.
- Sex toy boutique Babeland reported a 50 percent increase in sales in February, right around Valentine's Day.
- The sex toy market actually boomed during the recent recession.
- The top three sex toy states (based on per capita) are South Dakota, Idaho, and West Virginia.
- The three most popular purchases at sex toy stores are vibrators (19.2%), dildos (16%), and lube (14%). Well, that's boring.
- Sales in bondage toys reportedly increased by 50 percent after *50 Shades of Grey* became popular and Ben Wa balls, which are used for Kegel exercises, have had sales skyrocket by 350% because of the series.
- The band Steely Dan was named after a strap-on from the novel *Naked Lunch* by William S. Burroughs.

7.
There She Blows, There She Blows Again

It is vital you know about your most precious organ, the pretty peach. She is strong as she is fierce. She makes you. Treat her with respect, take care of her, and learn what makes her happy.

THE VAGINA MONOLOGUES

- ❖ A vaginal "fart," also called a "queef" or "vart," is common. Unlike gas expelled from the rectum, which contains fecal waste and has an odor, vaginal flatulence is odorless and unrelated to the rectum (unless a woman has a rare rectovaginal fistula).

- ❖ Each vagina has its own smell. The smell depends on a variety of factors, including the combination of normal bacteria that live in the vagina, diet, types of fabric a woman wears, level of hygiene, how much a woman sweats, and gland secretions.

- The recipe to the sensitivity of the clitoris is its 8,000 nerve fibers, which is twice as many as contained in the penis. As such, it is this area that most helps a woman reach orgasm. Men, rub the damn clit!! I'm only going to say that once.

- The first inch or two of the vagina has the most nerve endings and is the most pleasure receptive. If fellas are reading this…this stat is for you.

- The speculum (Latin for "mirror") dates back to 1300 B.C. Speculums have also been found in the ruins at Pompeii. Good to know they were practicing women's health back then.

- The first movie to use the word "vagina" on film was the 1946 Disney animated film called "The Story of Menstruation."

- The word "vagina" is Latin for "sheath" or "scabbard." The plural of vagina is vaginae or vaginas.

- One patient was so worried she had lost something in her vagina, she used pliers to try to find it. She ended up pulling on and tearing her cervix, which required hours of surgery to repair. Most gynecologists recommend that if a woman thinks something is in her vagina, to lube up the fingers with K-Y jelly or olive oil and stick them all the way inside. If she or her partner can't feel anything inside, chances are good that there's nothing there. A woman should not be embarrassed to call a gynecologist for help… My legs are shaking after that story.

❖ The pH balance of the vagina is around 4, which is the same pH as wine, tomatoes, and beer. Some things that change the pH of the vagina are vaginal infections, douching, soap, and exposure to semen.

❖ The largest vagina in history most likely belonged to Anna Swann (1846-1888). She was seven feet and five inches tall and weighed 350 pounds. She gave birth to a 23-pound baby with a 19-inch head.

❖ In 2006, in the novel *The Haunted Vagina*, a woman's vagina acted as a gateway to the world of the dead.

❖ In 2009, a healthy kidney designated for transplant was removed through the donor's vagina at John Hopkins Medical Center. This type of surgery is considered less invasive because the kidney was removed through a natural opening. The more traditional surgery typically requires a five to six-inch incision through the abdominal wall.

❖ Approximately one in 5,000-7,000 female babies are born without a vagina. Known as vaginal agenesis, the condition is sometime recognized at birth, but most of the time isn't diagnosed until puberty.

❖ Researchers believe that pubic hair evolved to become either a type of sexual ornament or as a way to trap pheromones.

❖ Hair around the vaginal area grows only for three weeks.

❖ Different vaginas have different smells at different times of the day. Right out of the shower, a vagina may not smell. After running or exercise, a vagina might smell musky from all the sweat glands. A menstruating vagina may smell like iron, and when a vagina has an overgrowth of yeast, it may smell like bread. After intercourse, a vagina may smell faintly like bleach, as semen has a smell of its own. If there is an overgrowth of bacteria, the vagina may smell like fish.

❖ The etymology of the word "cunt" is uncertain. Some scholars believe it derives from the Latin *cuneus*, "wedge," or from the Proto-Indo-European *gwen*, which is the root of "queen," and the Greek *gyne*, "woman."

❖ The vagina has over 1,000 nicknames, including "passion flower," "pink pearl," "ya-ya," "fish taco," "crotch mackerel," "cod canal," "fish factory," "fuzzy lap flounder," "tuna town," "penis penitentiary," "cum pocket," "yoni," "warehouse of warmth," "warm slurpee," the "V" thing," "apple pie," and "yum yum." What is your favorite word for the birthing canal?

❖ About 1 in 2,000 births, a girl is born with an imperforate hymen, which means there is no hole in the tissue to allow menses or discharge to pass through.

- Gynecologists say that there are natural ways to make a vagina smell fresher without douching, including: eliminate pubic hair, wipe with baby wipes instead of toilet paper, drink cranberry juice, which is a natural antibacterial, go panty free or wear cotton panties to keep the vagina aired out, take probiotics to keep vaginal flora healthy, avoid panty hose and tight jeans, and eat a healthy, vegetable-based diet. Foods such as coffee, asparagus, beets, alcohol, broccoli, onions, garlic, and curry can affect the smell.

- Painful sex (dyspareunia) is normal after a woman loses her virginity. But if the pain does not lessen and resolve after a while, other conditions may be involved, including vulvar vestibulitis (inflammation of the vestibule), vaginismus (involuntary contraction of the vaginal muscles), allergic reactions to things such as latex condoms or spermicide, and endometriosis (when lining from the uterus gets on the ovaries, bowel, and pelvic lining). As women age, lower levels of estrogen can cause atrophic vaginitis, or thinning of the vaginae.

- Most gynecologists believe that masturbating is healthy because it is safe sex, releases stress, a mood booster, and helps build pelvic floor muscles. However, there are exceptions. For example, one woman decided to masturbate with a banana. While masturbating, she put the stem side in first and lacerated her cervix, which required a hospital visit and stitches. If a woman puts something inside, she should stick to smooth fingers, vibrators, and dildos. Why though? Are we really that dumb in society?

- ❖ While each woman's vagina is different, the average length of an unaroused vagina in a mature woman is between 2.5-3.0 inches wide and 3.5 inches long. The vagina can expand up to 200 percent during sexual intercourse and giving birth.

- ❖ "Why do people say 'grow some balls'? Balls are weak and sensitive. If you wanna be tough, grow a vagina. Those things can take a pounding." This quote is usually attributed to Betty White, but comedian Sheng Wang actually said this.

- ❖ The hymen is named after Hymen, the Greek goddess of marriage, and is the membrane that partially covers the vagina. The hymen serves to project the vagina before puberty. After puberty and once estrogen thickens the vaginal tissue, the hymen serves little functional purpose.

- ❖ In some cultures, a woman's clitoris is cut off, the labia removed, and the vagina sewn shut, with the exception of a tiny hole (to allow for discharge). Widely condemned as genital mutilation, this horrific practice is done because it is believed it will make a woman more marriageable by both decreasing sexual desire and to ensure virginity. And I just shut my legs.

- ❖ *Vagina dentate* is Latin for "toothed vagina" and refers to the folktales in some cultures about women whose vaginas have teeth that can bite off a penis. Symbolically, the stories are told as a cautionary tales to discourage sexual behaviors. They can also prey on castration anxiety as well as the fear that men may be diminished by a woman. However, on rare occasions, dermoid cysts (which are cysts that can contain hair, brain, thyroid, skin, and teeth) can migrate their way to the vagina, which can cause *vagina denata*.

- Orgasms, along with sneezes, cannot be voluntarily stopped once they have started because they are physiological responses to an event. Thank God, I was worried there for a second.

- In a condition called pelvic prolapse, a woman's vagina can literally fall out and hang between the legs. Pelvic prolapse, however, can often be fixed. These are not pleasant facts.

- Some researchers believe that the G-spot (the Grafenberg spot) lies two to three inches inside the vagina, on the anterior wall (near the belly button), just under the urethra. They believe this area has a different texture than the rest of the vagina and may be a remnant prostate gland. Other researchers believe that the G-spot does not exist. What is your consensus?

- Trichomoniasis is a vaginal infection caused by a sexually transmitted parasite. Symptoms include itching, burning, and excess discharge that is bubbly, greenish or grayish, and may smell bad. Over 3.7 million people in the United States have the disease, though only 30 percent have symptoms.

❖ Bacterial vaginosis (BV) causes the classic fishy smell in a vagina and is sometimes associated with discharge, odor, pain, itching and burning. It is the most common vaginal infection in women of childbearing age. Researchers do not fully understand how a woman develops BV, but know it is associated with an imbalance of the bacteria that are normally found in a woman's vagina. Increased risk includes having a new sex partner or multiple partners and douching. A woman cannot get BV from toilet seats, bedding, or swimming pools, and women who have never had sexual intercourse can also be affected.

❖ While some cultures teach that vaginas are taboo or dirty places, one doctor notes that vaginas have also been celebrated through history and that "reclaiming the power and beauty is immensely liberating. Women, and the sexual distinctions that make us women, are the most powerful creative forces in the world." Additionally, studies show that women who are more confident about their vaginas have better orgasms.

❖ There are several vagina symbols, including oysters, fruits, flowers, handbags, and the vesica Pisces (the "vessel of the fish" that is often used as a Christ symbol).

❖ The vagina is a potential space, meaning that if nothing is holding it open, it collapses, like a sock without a foot in it.

- Both sharks and vaginas have a substance called squalene. Squalene exists in shark livers and is also a natural vaginal lubricant.

- The vagina begins at the opening of the vulva (from the Proto-Indo-European *wel-* "to turn, to revolve," and is related to *walzan* "to waltz") and ends at the cervix (from the Latin *cervix*, "the neck, nape of the neck").

- Inside the vagina is a series of ridges produced by folds of the vagina called the *vaginal rugae*. They allow the vagina to extend and stretch.

- The vagina is self-cleaning and, consequently, physicians discourage douching. The vagina has colonies of mutually symbiotic flora and microorganisms that protect against dangerous microbes. Disrupting this balance can cause yeast infections, abnormal discharge, and more.

- The vagina is not an open conduit to the abdominal cavity. While tiny, microscopic sperm can swim through the opening of the cervix, a tampon will never fit. So, it is impossible to lose a tampon, condom, or anything else in a vagina. Thank God!

- A 27-year-old woman in 2011 was charged with possession of heroin after 54 bags of the drug were found inside her vagina.

- While rare, it is possible for a woman to develop an allergy to the proteins in semen. This condition is known as human seminal plasma protein hypersensitivity. Most cases only involve itching and swelling after sex, but in some cases it can be life threatening. Research shows that certain women are allergic to certain men but not to others. So, it is possible to be allergic to douchebags? I knew it!

❖ One patient came to a gynecologist complaining that vines were coming out of her vagina. The doctor examined her and found that vines were indeed coming out. When the doctor removed the object, she found that it was a potato that had sprouted vines. The patient told the doctor that her mother told her to put a potato in her vagina to prevent pregnancy.

❖ While vaginal discharge can help lubricate the vagina, it is different from the vaginal lubrication produced during sex. The lube comes from special, pea-sized ducts called Bartholin's glands, which are located around the vaginal opening.

❖ Vaginas (like breasts, knees, and bottoms) can get saggy. Pregnancy, childbirth, age, hormonal changes, genetics, and years of gravity can weaken the supports of the female genital tract, which causes sagging. There are several ways to avoid sagging: Kegel exercises, maintaining a normal weight, avoiding constipation, and not smoking.

❖ Vaginal discharge does not contain any waste products. Instead, it contains the following: fluid that seeps through the walls of the vagina, cervical mucus, uterine and tubal fluid, secretions from glands in the vulva, oil and sweat from vulvar glands, old cells from the walls of the vagina, and healthy bacteria. Vaginal discharge contains mostly salt water, mucus, and cells.

- ❖ The average amount of vaginal discharge a woman of reproductive age secretes over a period of eight hours weighs 1.55 grams (1 gram=¼ teaspoon). Every woman makes different amounts of vaginal discharge, though it varies depending on where a woman is in her cycle. A woman procures the greatest amount of discharge (1.96 grams) around the time of ovulation.

- ❖ While vulvas typically vary between women, most vaginas look alike.

- ❖ One gynecologist reported that a patient of hers regularly used her vagina as a purse. The woman would stuff it with a plastic baggie of pills, a wad of bills, a tube of lipstick, and a pen. The woman later admitted that she had been sexually abused as an eight-year-old.

- ❖ According to one gynecologist, the most unusual vagina she had ever seen was on a woman who had come in for labor and delivery. She actually had two vaginas, with two cervixes. One cervix was eight centimeters dilated. The other was completely closed. She had had no prenatal care, but her husband had told her for years that having sex with her was like having sex with two different women.

- ❖ When one gynecologist was asked what it was like looking at vaginas all day, she replied "Really, it's just a bunch of different haircuts."

- ❖ One patient visited a gynecologist complaining of vaginal itching and feeling like "something is moving around inside." The examination revealed that there were two to three live maggots in her vagina. The gynecologists had no idea how the worms got into the vagina, but treated her with worming pills, cleaned the vagina, and told her not to put food products into her vagina.

- ❖ The vagina can stretch to THREE TIMES its original size—in girth—to accomplish this unmatched feat. The typical baseline diameter of a vagina is about 3 cm. An infant's head is around 10 cm across. You do the math.

- ❖ It can also grow nearly 50 percent in length. The vag is no slouch, herself. It lengthens during arousal, from an average length (i.e., depth) of 7 or 8 cm up to 10 or 11 cm.

- ❖ You can have two of them (sorta). Embryologically, the vagina forms from two tubular structures that fuse in the middle. The divider along the midline disappears during development. But occasionally it doesn't, so some women are born with a septum that divides the vagina into two. While some opt to have it removed, others may not even know it's there. It'll just push to one side or the other when inserting something, like a tampon, a penis or a dildo.

- The vagina is home to about 5 inches' worth of hidden clitoris. The clitoris is typically 9 to 11 cm long. Most of it is tucked out of view. "The most sensitive part is the clitoral glans—the part we see—but the entire thing, which extends into the vagina, can be stimulated," she explains, adding: "Take that!"

- There's no such thing as Whiskey Vagina. Sorry (not sorry).

- The clitoris is not a button — it's more like a wishbone. When most people think of the clitoris, they think of the small visible part. But research indicates that it actually has branches that extend down underneath the skin, along either side of the vulva, kind of in a wishbone shape. These branches can potentially be stimulated from the outside.

- Your vagina won't be noticeably different after you have babies. There is actually no statistical difference in average recorded vaginal size between women who've had babies and women who haven'.

- Feeling like you have to pee during sex, even though you *just* went? That's normal. About that clitourethrovaginal complex... Well, it can mean that sometimes your partner might be stimulating your urethra (or even bladder) during sex, which can potentially make you feel like you've gotta pee. There's also a thing called nerve cross-talk, which is where so much is going on down there that your nerves can become confused about what exactly they're experiencing. It might feel like you have to pee, but you're actually just becoming aroused.

- ❖ About half of all American women use vibrators. In a nationally representative study of 3,800 women between the ages of 18 and 60 in the United States, researchers found nearly half of the women had used a vibrator for masturbation, and 20 percent had done so within the past month. More than a third said they'd used one during intercourse, and 41 percent had used one during foreplay or sex play with a partner. Also, interesting 84 percent said they had used a vibrator externally, compared to 64% that had used one internally.

- ❖ Your birth control pill can impact how wet you're able to get, so can breastfeeding and menopause. That's because your vagina's ability to lubricate is partially tied to estrogen levels. The lower your estrogen levels, the harder it is to get wet naturally.

- ❖ About 30 percent of women felt some pain during their most recent sexual experience. There are some women who experience chronic pain from sex, like those who suffer from a condition called vulvodynia. But it is also incredibly common for women to occasionally and unpredictably feel pain while having sex — like if your partner rams your cervix, or if the fit is too tight, or you aren't quite lubricated enough. The good news is that most of these reasons are preventable.

❖ Lesbians report having more orgasms than straight or bisexual women. Why am I wasting my time with men again?

❖ The older you are, the less likely you are to remove your pubic hair. In a 2010 study of 2,451 women, researchers found that age was a major predictor of how much pubic hair women removed. For example, 18- to 24-year-olds were the most likely to report going totally hair-free; 25- through 49-year-olds were all most likely to list "some removal, not total"; and the majority of women over 50 said they didn't do any hair removal at all.

❖ Your vagina will actually let you know when you're most fertile. The cervical mucus will become clear and stretchy during ovulation, Dr. Dweck says. You'll probably also notice more of it than usual.

❖ Your vagina will also let you know if there's something wrong. Things to look out for is itching and irritation. Bloody discharge that isn't related to your period. Discharge that smells foul, or that is noticeably different from what you normally experience. Changes in smell, consistency, amount... If you're experiencing any of these symptoms, you should definitely go see a health care provider.

❖ Condoms will protect you against some STDs... but not all of them. Herpes and HPV can be spread from skin-to-skin contact, so it's still possible to contract either of these viruses even if you're incredibly diligent about condom usage.

- ❖ Other than abstinence, implants and IUDs are the most effective forms of reversible birth control. Worth noting: The implant and IUD do *not* protect against any STDs.

- ❖ You shouldn't have penetrative sex for about six weeks after you give birth. That's true whether you've had a vaginal birth or a C-section. There are a few reasons for it—most related to needing time to heal and avoiding infection.

- ❖ So many things can give you yeast infections. Sitting in a wet bathing suit or sweaty workout underwear. Drinking a lot of alcohol, or eating a ton of sugar. And being on antibiotics, because they can kill off all the good bacteria in your vagina and cause an imbalance that is hospitable to the fungus. Ick.

- ❖ The vagina is tilted at roughly a 130-degree angle, which is why you have to insert tampons by aiming them at your back. That said, things change with time. The vaginal angle flattens a bit, which may make vaginal intercourse feel different to women as they age and go through menopause.

THE DOWN AND DIRTY

Missionary. According to sex experts, women get the most pleasure out of basic missionary sex. There's nothing fancy about it, but women said they loved the closeness and the intimacy of having their partner's weight on them. In order for missionary position to be most effective, he needs to make sure he is entering her at the correct angle. Go in diagonally—rather than straight in and out—there's more friction for clitoral stimulation, which is best, since that's how most women achieve orgasm.

Reverse Cowgirl. In this position, the man is either lying down or in a sitting position, and the female straddles him backwards—facing his feet instead of his face. It's a key position that also allows easy access to the clitoris making it easier clitoral access, this position is the one that is most likely to facilitate an orgasm because direct clitoral stimulation is easy to engage in."

Doggie Style. Doggie style is a great position for the woman because it allows her to have optimal control. She is able to adjust her range of motion for an angle that feels best. He can likely stimulate her G-spot and have access to her clitoris with his hand, her hand or a toy. He needs to make sure to use his hands for clitoral stimulation too while in the doggie style position. She will rarely have an orgasm if he's not doing something manually in front at the same time.

Girl on Top. Another position that allows her to have the most control of her orgasm is when she's the one on top, facing forward. The position still needs to be a joint effort. He can help her by moving her hips up and down. It's a communication thing. When the woman is on top, she's in control of the depth and motion, as well as having easy access to her clitoris for pleasure.

Spooning. It concentrates on stimulation of the front portion of the vagina or rectum, which is where the most nerves are located in the genitals. Spooning is pleasurable because it creates a tighter fit in the vagina and rectum, so if a woman is looking for more stimulation from her partner's fingers or penis... spoon away.

Crisscross. Both partners are lying down. The woman is on her back and the guy is on his side. She has her legs draped over his middle like a giant X. Since your bodies aren't squished against each other, either you or she can reach down to rub her clitoris, what most women need to reach the Big O.

The Pillow Technique. Many sex experts agree that positions often become more pleasurable for a woman when a pillow or blanket is added to create a new angle of entry. In missionary. Put a pillow under her tush to give a pelvic lift. That can also help the man rub her g-spot with his penis. Certain angles for some women won't be comfortable. So, ask her what is working for her.

Coital Alignment Technique. This position is considered by many to be the "greatest sex position in the world." Start in a normal missionary position with the man's full body weight on top of the woman, not resting on his elbows. He moves forward so that the base of his penis is making direct contact with her clitoris. Her legs should be around his thighs and they should be moving together in a rhythmic, rocking motion. Some swear that this position allows for the closest physical connection and the best clitoral stimulation based on his positioning.

Ankles Up. The man has to put her ankles up over his shoulders. It allows him to go as deep inside of her as possible and hit her G-spot. The same deepness can also be achieved by her bending her knees or placing the soles of her feet on his chest.

A Single Girls Guide to...Hilarious Facts You Never Knew About Sex
WAIT...THERE'S HOW MANY??!!

Clitoral Orgasm. You know the external sweet spot is highly sensitive, thanks to the 8,000 nerve endings that congregate there. And if you're like most women, it's the go-to point of stimulation to send you over the edge.

Vaginal Orgasm. Though there is still some debate as to whether the G-spot exists, 30 percent of women claim they can have a big O from having the famous erogenous zone stimulated through penetration alone.

Blended Orgasm. Experts say a combined clitoral and vaginal orgasm is the most powerful finale (it can be twice as strong and intense as either orgasm is by itself).

Multiple Orgasms. To be clear, multiple orgasms happen one right after the next, not at different times in one session (although those are great too). Studies show that multiple orgasms are possible for some women if they can withstand being continuously stimulated after their first (and second and. . .) "Finishes." (I did not know that's what it meant...I don't think most guys know this either.) Also, I seriously want one of these.

The A–Spot Orgasm (The Anterior Fornix Orgasm). This kind of female orgasm is achieved by stimulation of an area deep in the vagina (about 4-5 inches) on the front wall. It is the same wall where the G-Spot is situated. In other words, this is a patch of sensitive tissue at the inner front end of the vaginal tube, between the cervix and the bladder. After an orgasm, the A-Spot does not become too sensitive, and you can easily continue stimulation, bringing your partner to new heights of pleasure, this is why women are able to achieve multiple orgasms. Many women find the feeling incredibly pleasurable, while some may not like it at all. Keep this in mind when experimenting.

The Deep Spot Orgasm (The Posterior Fornix Orgasm). This kind of female orgasm is achieved by stimulating the area located almost all the way back in the deepest part of the back wall of the vagina, just before the cervix. Direct stimulation of the Deep Spot can cause very intense orgasms. Some women may feel as if they are having anal sex. This particular area is not widely known, so very few women have ever experienced those sensations.

The U-Spot Orgasm. This kind of female orgasm comes from the stimulation of a small area of sensitive erectile tissue located just above and on either side of the urethral opening. It is in the small area between the urethra and the vagina. If this region is gently caressed with the finger, the tongue, or the tip of the penis, there is a powerful erotic response, you stimulate this area the same way you treat the clitoris.

The Breast Orgasm. This kind of female orgasm occurs during a peak of stimulation to the breasts. The nipples connect to nerves in the female genitals and many women feel a direct connection with their clitoris when their nipples are stimulated. Many women feel increased sexual excitement when their nipples are stimulated but not all of them can experience the breast orgasm. This depends very much on how sensitive their nipples are.

The Oral Orgasm. This orgasm can be experienced by women who are very sensitive orally. The mouth plays a big role in the sexual nervous system. The mouth orgasm can take place during any sensual oral activity such as kissing, licking, sucking, or performing oral sex. Many women describe the excitement as beginning in their lips and then spreading from the mouth to the genitals and all over the body.

The Skin Orgasm. This orgasm can be brought about by massaging certain areas of female body that are not directly connected to the sexual nervous system. Examples include orgasms experienced by many women during sensual massages.

The Mental Orgasm. This kind of female orgasm can happen during visual and auditory stimulation. Examples of such stimulation are movies, videos, or sexual behavior exhibited in front of others. Women become so turned on that they can actually experience an orgasm from the excitement alone.

A FEW MORE THINGS....

The majority of women can't orgasm from intercourse alone. Most women require clitoral stimulation, but because of the clitoris's location just outside the vagina, many don't receive the sensation they need for full arousal.

It's possible to have an orgasm and not know it. Not all orgasms involve the classic signs—sweating, rapid breathing, and muscle contractions. They can be much more subtle and mild, producing the sensation of gentle relaxation after arousal. Many women have bought into the "mind-blowing rockets and volcanos" model learned from romance novels and other unscientific sources.

Some orgasms are toe-curling and even transcendent, but some are gentle blips.

Orgasms don't happen in the genitals. They actually happen in the brain, which is possibly one reason that medications like selective serotonin reuptake inhibitors impact orgasm for so many users. We generally *feel* them in the genitals, and we'll feel a powerful orgasm all over the body. But the orgasm itself occurs in the brain. When the millions of nerve endings in the genitals are stimulated and aroused, they send messages to the nucleus accumbens, otherwise known as the brain's pleasure center.

Vibrators appeal to specific nerves. There's a reason vibrators are a popular choice for self-stimulation—the body has specialized nerves to perceive the sensation. Nerve endings adapt to all sorts of body functions and sensations. Sensing vibration is one of them." The most important consideration when using vibrators is safety: Make sure your sex toys are designed for the purpose for which you plan to use them, and always clean them with mild soap and warm water or a cleaner made specifically for sex toys.

Underwhelming orgasms can be caused by weak muscles. Pelvic floor health is an important part of sexual function. Weak pubococcygeus (PC) muscles can impact the strength of orgasm—another reason Kegel exercises are important. PC muscle contractions help us feel our orgasms. If the muscles are weak, the contractions don't feel like much, and it may feel like the orgasm didn't quite 'get there.'" Kegels strengthen the pelvic floor muscles that support the uterus, bladder, small intestine, and rectum, and regularly performing the discreet exercises can also aid in urinary incontinence. They're easy to do: Tighten the muscles that stop urination, then relax them for five seconds. Repeat several times in a row and work up to holding and relaxing for 10 seconds at a time. Try to perform at least 3 sets of 10 repetitions a day.

Orgasms are not an innate ability. Like crocheting or throwing a ball, nerves will actually grow to support one's ability to come. Some experts recommend relaxation exercises and Kegels, but it's important to talk to your health care provider if you feel a medical condition or medication may be hurting your ability to climax.

IT'S AN ORGASMIC EXPLOSION

- ❖ The word "orgasm" is from the Greek word *orgasmos*, which is defined as "to swell with moisture, be excited or eager."

- ❖ An orgasm is the "buildup of pleasurable body sensations and excitement to a peak intensity that then release tensions and creates a feeling of satisfaction and relaxation."

- ❖ Orgasms feel generally similar for men and women. The two body parts primarily involved in orgasms, the penis and clitoris, are homologous, meaning they both originate from the same tissue in the developing embryo. Additionally, the spinal cord and brain are connected to the penis and clitoris by the same nerve route.

- ❖ A brain on heroin looks similar to a brain during an orgasm

- Not all orgasms feel the same. Because the genitals are connected to several different pairs of nerves, stimulating different combinations of nerves produces different sensations. Additionally, orgasms are affected by cognitive, psychological, and pharmacological variables.

- Most researchers agree that Kegel exercises (named after gynecologist Arnold Kegel) increase the likelihood of orgasm. Kegels exercise the PC (pubococcygeus) muscles.

- Using condoms does not affect the quality of an orgasm.

- Anorgasmia means "lack of orgasm." This condition, where a person cannot achieve orgasm, can affect both men and women.

- According to Planned Parenthood, 30 percent of women have had trouble reaching an orgasm. As many as 80 percent have difficulty reaching orgasm through vaginal intercourse.

- Orgasms can be elicited from various regions of the body—including the penis, clitoris, vagina, G-spot, cervix, prostrate, nipples, breasts, and anus—as well as from visual stimulation, auditory stimulation, and mental imagery.

- Orgasms do not stop at a certain age. Some people can experience orgasms past the age of 90.

- The time it takes to reach an orgasm varies considerably. Orgasm also depends on a variety of factors such as age, sexual experience, and drugs.

Men typically require 2–10 minutes to reach orgasm. While women typically require a more prolonged period of stimulation before an orgasm (often 20 minutes), some women can have an orgasm within 30 seconds of self-stimulation.

❖ In one study, women's orgasms lasted 18 seconds on average, and men's orgasms lasted about 22 seconds. Another study found that a woman's orgasms last about 3–15 seconds, while a man's orgasm is shorter. I feel like this statistic is in here before but I can't find. Hey, repetition is how you remember.

❖ Multiple factors influence exactly how long it will last, including age, period of sexual abstinence, type of sexual stimulation, and whether the orgasm is from masturbation or intercourse.

❖ In one study, 85 percent of men reported that their partner had an orgasm. However, only 64% of their female partners reported experiencing an orgasm, creating what some sexologists call an "orgasm gap." That means 20 percent of women fake it, stop it!

❖ The duration of an orgasm tends to decrease as a person ages.

❖ While orgasms usually result from genital stimulation, orgasm can occur from non-genital stimuli as well, including thinking of an orgasm; orgasms experienced during meditation; orgasms produced by stimulating any part of the body, including mouth, lips, nipples, anus, shoulder, or toe; orgasms during childbirth; orgasms during defecation and "forceful urination; and one woman reported having orgasms while brushing her teeth.

- There is a clear relationship between a woman's age and the likelihood she'll experience an orgasm. In a 1994 U.K. study of 436 women, 63 percent of women 35-39 years old experienced orgasm during more than half of or all of their sexual interactions. Only 21 percent of women 55-59 reported this frequency. Five percent of the younger women but 35 percent of the older women had not experienced an orgasm at all.

- Orgasms have been reported by stimulation after male-to-female or female-to-male transsexual surgery.

- Non-genital orgasms have been reported by people who are under the influence of psychedelic drugs.

- People who experience orgasms often look like they are pain. In fact, two of the brain regions that are activated by pain are also activated during orgasm, perhaps accounting for the curious similarity of facial expressions. Scientists are unsure how the brain distinguishes between pain and pleasure.

- For some women, stimulation of the nipples and breasts can increase the likelihood of having an orgasm and increase its intensity.

- The world record for a woman masturbating to orgasm is six hours and 30 minutes. The world record for man masturbating to orgasm is eight hours and 30 minutes.

- ❖ Orgasms can relieve pain, albeit for only about 8–10 minutes afterwards. However, even thinking about sex can relieve pain.

- ❖ Approximately 47 percent of women experienced their first orgasm through masturbation. The average age to experience it is 18. I was a bit younger…

- ❖ During sex, vaginal lubricant seeps into the vagina canal from blood capillaries in the vaginal lining. Antihistamines may interfere with vaginal lubrication in the same way they inhibit a runny nose.

- ❖ Female ejaculation is not urine (though women may expel urine during an orgasm). It resembles diluted fat-free milk and has a sweet taste. Although the volume may seem large during an orgasm, the total amount of liquid released during an orgasm usually is not over 1 teaspoon (4 ml). Squirting is not piss! I knew it!

- ❖ Women who feel less secure in their relationship are less likely to orgasm.

- ❖ Aristotle is considered to be the first to write about female ejaculation. Galen, the famous Greco-Roman physician and philosopher, also knew about it in the 2nd century AD.

- Before restrictions were imposed on this type of research, orgasms were produced by direct electrical or chemical stimulation of the brain.

- Orgasms have been reported unexpectedly by electrical stimulation of the spine, initially done for pain control.

- Orgasms can be produced in women and men with spinal cord injuries by a loved one caressing hypersensitive non-genital skin zones near the site of their injury.

- Body positions during vaginal intercourse can affect orgasm in women.

- The French refer to an orgasm as the *le petit mort*, "the little death."

- While most couples say the penis size does not affect a woman's orgasm, some women say the length and, most importantly, the girth of a penis is important. However, just as penises vary in size and shape, so do vaginas. Size preference, or the idea of a "good fit," is hard to generalize.

- Researchers note that a woman might be more likely to become pregnant if she has an orgasm. An orgasm increases a suction produced by wave-like contractions of the uterus that draw in ejaculated semen that has been deposited near the cervix.

- Women sometimes experience orgasms while giving birth. These orgasms have been called "birth-gasms."

- Studies show that the application of a transdermal androgen patch, which is designed to release low amounts of testosterone through the skin and into the bloodstream, has positive effects on a woman's orgasm and sexual satisfaction. This is especially true for postmenopausal women, women who have had their ovaries removed, and women who have an androgen-insufficiency disorder.

- Scientists have created a neuro-stimulation device for woman that can deliver remote-controlled orgasms.

- Ejaculation and orgasm don't necessarily require an erection. Many men who have had surgery for prostate cancer are able to experience orgasm without an erection.

- Scientists are unsure why some men experience significantly increased sensitivity and even pain of the penis after orgasm.

- Both men and women can delay orgasm through a variety of ways. For example, in some practices of Hinduism—such as Tantra, which emphasizes sexual intercourse for religious purposes—techniques allow some individuals to control ejaculation and orgasm.

- Men can have an orgasm without the stimulation of his penis. In fact, most men have experienced an orgasm while asleep (aka a wet dream). Additionally, in rare cases (three or four men out of 5,000), men have had an orgasm without tactile

- stimulation while awake. (Wasn't that in American Pie? Is that getting too excited?)

- ❖ Some men who practice a specialized form of rapid breathing and Tantric meditation ("fire breath") reportedly have experienced orgasm without physical genital stimulation.

- ❖ Ancient Egyptians believed that the god Atum created the world through masturbating and that the Tigris River was formed by the semen of a god.

- ❖ A recent study shows that the ability to climax may be linked to genetics.

- ❖ The clear fluid that comes out of the penis before ejaculation is called pre-ejaculate. It can be so abundant as to fill 1/5 of a teaspoon. Medieval writers called it "the distillate of love."

- ❖ Different types of illegal and legal drugs affect orgasms in both positive and negative ways. Steroids (especially testosterone), Yohimbine, cocaine, and dopamine have positive or stimulating effects on orgasms. On the other hand, antidepressant drugs have a negative effect.

- ❖ While orgasms are felt in the brain, the orgasmic process involves virtually every body system. Researchers note that the brain is the "conductor of the orgasmic orchestra."

- ❖ The book *The Fundamentals of Sex* claims that it is possible for some women to experience orgasms up to 100 times in an hour.

- The Prague Sex Machines Museum has over 200 objects and machines, including some from hundreds of years ago, that have helped people achieve orgasms and sexual satisfaction.

- At least eight species of female primates show signs that they experience orgasms.

- No one knows with certainty why some men become so sleepy after an orgasm. A 175-pound man participating in vigorous sex for 30 minutes expends a mere 63 calories. If he had spent the same time jogging, he would have used 288 calories. Researchers speculate the brain releases chemicals, such as prolactin, which causes sleepiness. On the other hand, women report feeling less tired than men after an orgasm.

- An orgasm burns just 2–3 calories, though a person can burn around 50 calories in the activity leading up to the orgasm.

- Seventy percent of coital deaths have occurred during extramarital intercourse.

- Orgasms can also cause headaches known as "orgasmic headaches." Physicians note that these are similar to headaches after exercise and are caused by a temporary rise in blood pressure and muscle spasms of the neck and scalp.

- San Francisco's Center for Sex & Culture organizes an annual masturbate-a-thon. The participants meet at the center and masturbate for charity. Why? And for what charity? That's kind of creepy.

- A hysterectomy may affect a woman's' ability to have an orgasm. While the nerves that convey sensation from the clitoris are likely to remain undamaged, the nerves that convey sensation from the vagina are more likely to be damaged.

- According to one study, clitoral piercing does not negatively affect orgasm. If done correctly. If done wrong it could damage nerves.

- Using the term "achieve" to describe an orgasm may put pressure on sexual partners to always achieve an orgasm. Sexual health experts use the word "experience" instead.

- The record for the most female orgasms in a single masturbation session was reportedly 49 from a woman in London in 2006. I stop after three or four.

- Scientists can infer a woman's history of vaginal orgasm by the way she walks. How can you tell by the way she walks?

- Research indicates that 67 percent of women fake orgasm. Way too many ladies! Stop! It benefits no one.

- According to a University of Kansas survey in 2009, about 25 percent of men reported faking an orgasm. It's that high? That's one in four.

- Some scientists believe that not every woman has a G-spot. The G-spot is typically believed to be located 1–2 inches up on the inside wall of the vagina. It is usually pea-sized but can grow to be the size of a walnut. Here it is again… So, what is it???

- ❖ Almost all women who could reach orgasm before cancer treatments can do so after treatments.

- ❖ That spark or jolt up your spine that you sometimes feel when aroused is the pudendal nerve, which connects the penis/clitoris to the brain.

- ❖ The penis and clitoris, are homologous, aka they form from the same tissue in a developing embryo.

- ❖ People have reported orgasming from simply thinking about orgasming.

- ❖ Former U.S. Vice President Nelson A. Rockefeller died after suffering a heart attack during sex with a woman in a hotel room.

- ❖ Circumcision doesn't negatively affect a man's ability to achieve orgasm, but foreskin does seem to lead to increased duration.

- ❖ As an orgasm becomes imminent in a woman, the vagina decreases in size by as much as 30%. This contraction is most likely to help increase the sensitivity felt by the woman as she climaxes into the orgasm.

- ❖ The amygdala, the part of your brain triggering fear and anxiety, shuts down when women have an orgasm.

- Having an orgasm releases an anti-diuretic hormone, which is why you probably find yourself not being able to pee right after sex.

- Forty percent of women have experienced exercise-induced orgasms on more than 11 different occasions. I would really like to know what exercises they were doing? Thank you. And you might have to describe in detail. Also, what machines are the best to do that?

- Older women are more likely to say they'd orgasmed during their last sexual encounter than younger women. Well, that's because they have been around the block a few times and know their body. That is not a surprising fact. Also, younger women tend to fake it. Please stop. Men should not be put on a pedestal.

- It tends to be easier for women to orgasm during ovulation than at any other time in their cycle. So basically, only four days a month? Cool.

- For up to 70 percent of women, simultaneous direct stimulation of the clitoris during intercourse is essential for them to reach orgasm. The other 30% have never experienced this. (Meaning they have probably never orgasmed.)

- In rare cases, menstrual cramps have been known to bring about orgasm. I'm going to think that way the next time I have menstrual cramps, that it's just an orgasm.

- Approximately 30 percent of women have orgasms from vaginal intercourse. Some researchers claim that a vaginal orgasm may be a deep clitoral orgasm. Other researchers claim that vaginal and clitoral orgasms are completely different and activate different parts of the brain. The word orgasm is from the Proto-Indo-European root *wrog*, meaning "to burgeon, swell with strength."

❖ Roughly 16 percent of women say they've never had an orgasm during intercourse. And from the same study, about 20 to 30 percent of women say they only reached orgasm during sex about one in four times...or fewer.

❖ To increase your odds of having an orgasm, mix it up in bed. Research from the NSSHB shows that women who combine a variety of sex "acts" in one session (as in penetration + hands + oral) are more likely to report having orgasms than people who just stick to one sex act.

CHAPTER 8
Everybody Masturbates... Sometimes

FEELING MYSELF

❖ Vibrators were apparently created by Cleopatra. It was basically an empty gourd full of bees. She was such an innovator. I just want to say what a BAMF she really was. We don't talk enough about this vixen.

❖ Some French aristocrat, who's a pervert, named Marquis de Sade (1740-1814), is the godfather of sadomasochism. He masturbated into a chalice in front of a prostitute while antagonizing God.

❖ This might be my favorite, and obviously most logical story of the creation of the world. In Egyptian Mythology, there was a lone God named Atum, who masturbated and that is how our world came to be. There's also something in there about him drowning a nun too, but that's neither here nor there.

- ❖ I can't with these. Masturbation used to be a historical symbol of Abundance? Not joking. Ancient Middle Eastern pagans would engage in orgiastic mutual masturbation sessions during the harvest. The key was to ejaculate at the same time, therefore summoning beneficent energies from the gods of life and land.

- ❖ The masturbatory art of Jelqing supposedly originated in the ancient Middle East. This form of masturbation was used for penis enlargement. Haha, I wondered if it works. It sounds like manual manipulation and broken blood vessels. That sounds appetizing.

- ❖ In Taoism, sex should only take place if a woman is aroused. Similarly, Renaissance artists often depicted women with sex toys and in provocative sexual positions to emphasize fertility.

- ❖ Also, in Taoism, "single cultivation" occurs when a man masturbates, and instead of ejaculating his "jing," his maleness is converted to "qi" (energy), and then absorbed into the spine and turned into "shen" (spiritual power). Apparently, don't do that it is very bad for you. It hurts your liver, kidneys, and like most women who don't pee after sex, there will be a urinary tract infection.

- ❖ The Latin etymology of the word masturbate references "defilement," "dishonor," and "hand." ☺ The ancient Romans were nonchalant joked about masturbation. Ancient Pompeii graffiti read "when my worries oppress by body, with my left hand, I release my pent-up fluids."

- There was the Victorian hand-crank of the 1890s, a steam-powered contraption named "The Manipulator" made by an American doctor. There was also an electromechanical vibrator made first by Dr. Granville to help with Victorian "hysteria."

- Oh, the Victorian era and its hysteria, Doctor's would do a vaginal massage to help cure them☺ Now that's my kind of doctor, when I'm feeling sick.

- Masturbation is the most common sexual activity. (I'm gonna go with a "Duh" on that one.)

- Pee Wee Herman was arrested for masturbating in an X-rated movie theater.

- "If God had intended us not to masturbate, He would have made our arms shorter." – George Carlin

- Masturbation is 100 percent safe. Haha, did you know that? Unless you slip in the shower and break your penis.

- May is International Masturbation Month. If I would have known that, I would have made it my mission to Masturbate at least once a day. It is August as I write this, and I am very disappointed in myself.

- Eighteenth Century Scottish men would actually drink beer talk and masturbate together. Yeah, so do any of my girlfriends want to come over and watch Magic Mike, drink Mojitos, and pillow fit?

- Ancient Greek women would actually masturbate to bread sticks. Now I can finally get into baking☺

- Pharaohs used to masturbate in the Nile. That is now on my bucket list.

- Cave porn was found in Australia. Porn dates back over 28,000 years ago. I am not a big fan of porn if I do say myself. I like the softcore and fantasy.

- Romans only masturbate with their left hands.

- Most importantly masturbation reduces stress.

- Masturbation helps you get to sleep, get rid of a headache, boost the immune system, prevent diabetes, prevent cystitis, help make you more sexually confident. Why don't we masturbate more often? I always have a fantasy man, Joe Manganiello, I highly recommend. Sorry Sofia, I am allowed, plus I am a rat in Chinese year like you, so if you guys' divorce, I will be right there in the wings.

- The oldest-reported dildo is 30,000 years old and was unearthed in a German cave.

- Ancient Greeks had *olisbokollikes* ("dildo breadsticks") since 400 B.C.

- One of the first vibrators, The Tremoussoir, was invented in France in 1734.

- The first electric vibrator is credited to be invented by Dr. Joseph Mortimer Granville to relieve muscle aches. It weighed 40 pounds, required two people to operate, and that's not including the recipient.

- ❖ Vibrators were initially used by doctors to cure hysteria in women, the symptoms for which included "anxiety, sleeplessness, irritability, nervousness, erotic fantasies, feelings of heaviness in the lower abdomen, and wetness between the leg."

- ❖ The first electric vibrator was officially patented by Hamilton Beach in 1902. It was the first domestic appliance that was electrified after the sewing machine, tea kettle, toaster, and fan.

- ❖ However, to be discreet, vibrators were advertised as "personal massagers."

- ❖ After the 1920s, when vibrators started making appearances in pornographic films, the devices were pulled from advertisements well into the 1970s.

- ❖ And it's illegal to own more than six dildos in Texas.

- ❖ Fifty-two percent of women have used a vibrator before.

- ❖ One in three American women owns a vibrator.

- ❖ Women who used vibrators scored higher on the Female Sexual Function Index scale.

- ❖ Studies show that women who use sex toys tend to be more consistent with getting pelvic exams and caring about their vaginal health.

- Dildo replicas exist of famous porn stars like James Deen and Ron Jeremy and other celebs. I don't know why you would want Ron Jeremy's penis, but that is neither here nor there.

- There's a company called Bad Dragon that manufactures dragon-themed dildos, adult accessories, and more. I know I WANT to have sex with a dragon…

- The most expensive sex toy in the world is a white gold vibrator with 117 embedded diamonds, worth $55,000.

- The Rabbit vibrator was invented in 1983 and was made to look like a rabbit because Japanese manufacturers weren't actually allowed to make vibrators.

- *Sex and the City* writers decided to give Charlotte an obsession with the Rabbit after going to the Pleasure Chest and learning that the Rabbit was their best-selling toy.

- In 2006, Oprah dubbed The Rabbit Habit as the "Rolls Royce of sex toys."

- About 400 BP, the term "dildo" made its way into the vernacular of Renaissance Italy, with penis-shaped--often exaggerated-in-size and including testicles--bedroom buddies becoming popular features of *boudoirs* all across Europe. Linguistically derived from the Greek term "oblisbo" (in Latin, "to open wide,") dildos of this era were commonly made of wood or leather, with diaries from the period explaining that liberal amounts of olive oil were needed for easy insertion.

- ❖ In November 2013, someone in Japan combined virtual reality goggles with a robotic arm. At the time, it was described as a "sort of wonderful masturbating Voltron." The Guardian Express opined that as far as sex toys, it may be "perhaps the most sophisticated one the world has ever seen." We can likely assume that we have been using sex toys for as long as we have been walking upright … and maybe even before that time.

- ❖ Chimpanzees, our closest primate relatives, for example, use a number of tools in everyday life, including a version of a dildo for sexual gratification.

- ❖ Masturbation is known to help cure depression as the release of emotions and hormones when orgasm is reached to put your mind at ease, and make you more comfortable with your own body.

- ❖ OhMiBod Vibrator. The OhMiBod is a way for all of us to climax along with the latest Beyoncé single, and who wouldn't want that? Now that being said…

A Single Girls Guide to...*Hilarious Facts You Never Knew About Sex*

IT'S JUST ME AND MY HAND TONIGHT

- Genuine – Pony
- Michael Jackson – Dirty Diana
- Michael Jackson – Give in to Me
- Bad Company – Feel like Making Love
- Foreigner – Feels like the First Time
- Awolnation – Sail
- The Black Keys – Howling for You
- Britney Spears – Breathe on Me
- Britney Spears – Early Morning
- Chris Cornell – Scream
- Christina Aguilera – Infatuation
- Madonna – La Isla Bonita
- Lana Del Rey – Dark Paradise
- Mirah – The Garden
- Remy Zero – Prophecy
- Rihanna – S & M
- Rihanna – Roc Me Out
- Truth Hurts Feat. Rakim – Addictive

- Usher – Hot Tottie
- 50 Cent – Just a lil Bit
- Yael Naim – Toxic
- Felix Da Housecat – Silver Screen
- Destiny's Child – Lose My Breath
- Lil Kim – How Many Licks
- Sofia Karlberg – Crazy in Love
- Blue Foundation – Eyes on Fire
- Melanie Fiona – Give it To Me Right
- Prince – Darling Nikki
- The Pussycat Dolls – Buttons
- The Weeknd – Worth It
- Chris Isaak – Wicked Games
- Nine Inch Nails – Closer
- Janet Jackson – If
- Pink – Fingers
- Fiona Apple – Criminal
- Toni Braxton – You're makin' me high
- Portishead – Glory Box
- Madonna – Justify My Love

- 112 – Anywhere
- Pretty Ricky – Grind With me
- Jeremih – Birthday Sex
- Alex Clare – Damn Your Eyes
- Jimmy Eat World – Goodbye Sky Harbor
- Jimmy Eat World – For Me this is Heaven
- Jimmy Eat World – Just Watch the Fireworks
- Justin Timberlake – Like I love you
- INXS – Tear Us Apart
- Selena Gomez – Good for you
- Annie Lennox – I Put a Spell on You
- Celine Dion – Seduces Me
- Katie Kadan – All Better
- Whethan and Dua Lipa – High
- Tove Lo – Vibes
- Imagine Dragons – Believer
- Two Feet – Fell Like I'm Drowning
- Two Feet – Go Fuck Yourself
- Matt Maeson – Put it on Me
- Tyga – Taste

- ❖ Claudia Kane – Under My Skin
- ❖ JX Riders and Skylar Stecker – Sweet Dreams

Other Books by Sarah Melland

THE BREAKUP BAND AID/THE BREAKUP BAND AID WORKBOOK

This "How Not To" book gives you everything you supposedly need in a breakup book. Plus, helpful insights as to how not to have a nervous breakdown or a restraining order. It will make you laugh out loud, cry uncontrollable tears, get in shape, travel around the world, and make you glow like the shining confident person you were always meant to be.

ROMANCES OF A SAIF IN LA

In Romances of a SAIF: Beginner's Guide will introduce what is a SAIF, how to SAIF, how to feign confidence, gain self-respect, build your self-worth, be independent, forgive yourself and so much more. It will chronicle what type of men to steer clear of on dating apps and where else to meet them organically.

PRACTICING LOVE/JOURNAL EDITION

Practicing Love will help you meditate with ease, turn your mind off to distractions, and open your world of possibilities with easy tips you can incorporate into your everyday busy life. It goes into depth about how the ego makes you operate out of fear and shows you how to turn that negative mindset into one that empowers you to conquer obstacles by getting out of your comfort zone. It goes through simple descriptions of all the universal laws that will help you live a more positive, happy, and fulfilled life. It gives you hundreds of affirmations you can recite when you are feeling down in any scenario. It will also show you which words you need to eliminate from your vocabulary immediately and how to start talking in manifestation mode 24/7. It has tons of exercises to help you live in the present moment, become more patient, support yourself in forgiving yourself and others, become less selfish, not react out of judgement, and finally, to always feel unconditionally loved.

PRACTICING LOVE GRATITUDE JOURNAL

Practicing Love Gratitude Journal is 365 days of writing prompts that will take you through all the spiritual laws of attraction and how to show grace in your everyday lives. It allows you to go deep within yourself through daily reflection, shows you what you have been resisting and teaches you how to flip the switch. It will help you heal on numerous levels, relieve stress, anxiety, self-doubt, and ultimately aid in conquering your fears through forgiveness and perseverance. You will create easy, attainable every day goals by setting your intentions and maximizing manifestation throughout the day. You will also learn how to break free from your ego mindset, discover your self-worth, and realize what a truly magical person you really are. May your life be filled with the vibration of love, and always remember to write from a place of gratitude.

Instagram: @yourdatingunexpert

www.sarahmelland.com

References

Henry, Ben. "24 Facts About Lube You Should Really Know" *Buzzfeed,* January 16, 2016. https://www.buzzfeed.com/benhenry/lube-it-up-lube-it-up

Schupak, Amanda. "15 Vagina Facts That Would Make Penises Jealous." *Self,* January 6, 2016. https://www.self.com/story/15-vagina-facts-that-would-make-penises-jealous

Lehnardt, Karin. "50 Surprising Vagina Facts." *Fact Retriever,* September 2, 2016. https://www.factretriever.com/vagina-facts

Nelson, January. "30 Strange But Interesting Facts About The Penis Your Boyfriend Probably Doesn't Even Know." *Thought Catalog,* February 1st 2018. https://thoughtcatalog.com/january-nelson/2018/02/31-strange-but-interesting-facts-about-the-penis-your-boyfriend-probably-doesnt-even-know/

Stuber, Chris. "22 Facts about Penises That You Didn't Know (But Always wanted to)." *Buzznick,* May 22, 2019. https://www.buzznick.com/penis-facts/

Varina, Rachel. "36 Hilarious, Need-To-Know Facts About Oral Sex That You (And Your Boyfriend) Should REALLY See" *Total Sorority Move,* January 30, 2016. https://totalsororitymove.com/36-hilarious-need-to-know-facts-about-oral-sex-that-you-and-your-boyfriend-should-really-see/

Dutta, Sharangee. "20 Interesting Facts About Kissing That Prove It's More Than Just A Passionate Moment." *Scoop Whoop.* https://www.scoopwhoop.com/facts-about-kissing/

Lehnardt, Karin. "48 Kissing Facts." *Fact Retriever,* November 22, 2016. https://www.factretriever.com/kissing-facts.

Kylstra, Carolyn. "29 Things Everyone With A Vagina Should Definitely Know." *Buzzfeed,* October 23, 2014. https://www.buzzfeed.com/carolynkylstra/vagina-facts
"The Most Weird and Odd Sex Facts You Shouldn't Miss" *Enki Village.* http://www.enkivillage.com/weird-sex-facts.html

Zalta Thoughts. "50 Crazy Sex Facts for the Modern Woman That'll Fascinate & Educate You" *She Knows*, March 28, 2018 http://www.sheknows.com/love-and-sex/articles/996875/50-crazy-sex-facts-for-the-modern-women

Driscoll, Brogan. "17 Sex Facts that Will Make you Laugh, Gasp (Not In A Good Way) And Possibly Vomit #NSFW" *The Huffington Post UK*, December 4, 2015. http://www.huffingtonpost.co.uk/2013/09/18/sex-facts-will-make-you-laugh_n_3946265.html

Fortey, Ian. "The 25 Most Disturbing Sex Toys" *Cracked*, March 18, 2008 http://www.cracked.com/article_16032_the-25-most-disturbing-sex-toys_p2.html

Morris M. "Sex Toys With Ridiculousy Ancient Origins" *ListVerse*, October 26, 2019. http://listverse.com/2013/01/11/10-sex-toys-with-ridiculously-ancient-origins/

Pugachevsky, Julia. "33 Facts You Never Knew About Sex Toys." *Buzzfeed*, July 10, 2014. http://www.buzzfeed.com/juliapugachevsky/facts-you-never-knew-about-sex-toys#.jkJozZbxLR

Rosenthal, Martha. "Masturbation: A Brief and Rigorous History" *Psychology Today*, June 25, 2012. https://www.psychologytoday.com/blog/get-psyched/201206/masturbation-brief-and-rigorous-history

Caster, Yvette. "The history of sex toys and masturbation in 10 fascinating facts." *Metro,* May 14, 2015. http://metro.co.uk/2015/05/14/the-history-of-sex-toys-and-masturbation-in-10-fascinating-facts-5195377/

"11 Different Types of Orgasms." *Monica's Box,* July 15, 2012. https://monicasbox.wordpress.com/2012/07/15/11-different-types-of-orgasms/

Lampen, Claire. "10 Orgasms Every Woman Should Have." *Women's Health*, October 2, 1018. http://www.womenshealthmag.com/sex-and-love/types-of-female-orgasm

www.ingramcontent.com/pod-product-compliance
Lightning Source LLC
Chambersburg PA
CBHW071857070526
44583CB00016B/1725